Pastors
—— Are ——
People
Too

What people are saying about …

Pastors Are People Too

"The intersection of faith and leadership is a dangerous place! Our pastors live where kingdoms collide, and all too often they are on a solo journey. After reading *Pastors Are People Too*, I'm now resourced and prepared to be a better layperson, a better supporter, and a much better friend. I believe God is pleased with that."

Rob McCleland, president of John
Maxwell Leadership Foundation

"As I have coached hundreds of pastors in the last decade and looked deeply into my own heart, I can see that pastors have a huge need: encouragement! We need people around us who we know are for us regardless of whether our sermon is great or our leadership is inspiring. We need people to say 'I love you' because of who you are and not just what you do. *Pastors Are People Too* could start a revolution for leaders in local churches to love their pastors better."

Dr. Darrin Patrick, lead pastor of The Journey,
St. Louis, vice president of Acts 29, and author of
Church Planter and *The Dude's Guide to Marriage*

"The American way of doing church has created immense pressure on pastors. Jimmy Dodd's new book, *Pastors Are People Too*, is a godsend, literally, not just to pastors, but also to their spouses, elder boards, and congregations. This timely book opens up a desperately needed conversation on how to pastor and enjoy the journey!"

Floyd McClung, founder of All Nations, Cape Town

"Few understand the unique experience of us pastors and our loved ones like Jimmy Dodd and Larry Magnuson. Writing from the perspectives of an experienced pastor and counselor to pastors, the authors identify several unique struggles that if better known by our people would encourage them to support us well in our calling. Jimmy and Larry don't merely understand these struggles; they also give our people the understanding, opportunity, and tools they need to empower and strengthen us in our calling. Consider *Pastors Are People Too* your how-to manual for pastoring your pastor."

Scott Sauls, senior pastor of Christ Presbyterian Church, Nashville, and author of *Jesus outside the Lines*

"Critical topics for all pastors, a must read for all church leadership wanting to build a healthy and effective church."

Keith Cote, vice president of Lead222, speaker, author, and coach

"This book is a much-needed wake-up call to the church to care for its pastors in this age of workaholism and unending expectations on leaders. As experts at shepherding pastors, the authors share helpful stories to illustrate the incredible complexity of pastoring and provide insights on how we can champion our church leaders. This book challenges all of us to steward our lives more fully to the Lord."

Dr. Tasha D. Chapman, director of
educational studies at Covenant Theological
Seminary and coauthor of *Resilient Ministry*

"When the pastor is healthy and focused, the church has far greater potential to be healthy and focused. *Pastors Are People Too* should be required reading for every church leader who wants to see their church thrive."

David Kinnan, lead pastor of
Fountain Springs Church

"Pastor Jimmy has written a beautifully simple and practical book that addresses the often-overlooked ministry of providing pastoral care for our pastors. I believe that healthy churches depend on healthy leaders who are loved and supported by their communities. This ultimately leads to a beautiful expression of the gospel in our cities all around the world. Thank you, Jimmy, for such an important work!"

Kevin Palau, president of Luis Palau
Association and author of *Unlikely*

"Many of my heroes and best friends throughout life have been pastors—and I have been a pastor myself. So I'm glad this book is bringing to light the challenges these servants often face, as well as equipping us with practical ways to support them and help lighten their load. I can't think of anyone more passionate about this and more qualified to bring us this message than Jimmy and Larry."

Carey Casey, CEO of National
Center for Fathering

"Every pastor needs an advocate, defending, protecting, and celebrating their ministry. In this book, Jimmy Dodd is urging the pastor's most likely group—their congregation—to provide what is often assumed to be happening, but more often is neglected: prayerful, practical, and proactive care of their pastor. It's not rocket science, but it's amazing how even the simplest common courtesies are consistently missed by those who are faithfully served by today's pastoral leader."

Stephen Macchia, founding president
of Leadership Transformations, director
of the Pierce Center at Gordon-Conwell
Theological Seminary, and author of *Becoming
a Healthy Church* and *Broken and Whole*

"Dodd brings a very unique and priceless background to this book. He has been a pastor (over twenty years) and he has counseled hundreds of pastors who were dealing with every imaginable problem from crises that destroyed their ministries to naïveté that portended future problems. His is a hard-won perspective that is invaluable. It says to the reader your pastor is not the exception; he will have certain problems if you and your church leadership don't champion his cause."

Jim Cavnar, president of Cross International

"Finally a book that addresses the profession of pastor with dignity. This is a great weave of the personal journey of the writer as well as the many with whom the writer has served coupled with deeper understanding of the dilemmas but also the answers on moving forward. This brings life, transparency, and reality to the pages. Hope as well as directives for growth ring loud and clear. All church leaders need this for inspiration and instruction. We have greatly benefited from the ministry of PastorServe."

Jo Anne Lyon, general superintendent
of the Wesleyan Church

"Pastors need help, and SonScape Retreats has been helping thousands of them in powerful ways for decades. That's why we've served on SonScape's board for a quarter century. And that's why we're so excited to see Larry and Jimmy's new book, which can sensitize believers to the struggles their pastors face and help them contribute to healthier pastoral lifestyles and healthier churches!"

Lois and Steve Rabey, SonScape Retreats

"This book is designed to help church members help their pastor. Pastors are people too. The title is true. But not everybody wants to see it that way. Many pastors and their families feel isolated and cut off—both personally and ministerially—from the very supports and nourishment they give to their congregations. Asking for help is seen by too many as a sign of weakness, so those who need counseling the most avoid it. Jimmy and Larry offer a principled approach to congregational health that starts with the health of congregational leaders, especially the pastor and his family. The chapter on the wife of a pastor is worth the price of the book alone, as well as the chapter on pastors' kids. This book flows out of decades of ministry to pastors and their families and is valuable for developing congregational leadership, pastors continuing their education, and training of future pastors."

Wade Mobley, pastor, president of the Free
Lutheran Schools, and dean of the Association
Free Lutheran Theological Seminary

"Calling all sheep! You have worn your shepherds ragged and it has to stop—for their sakes and for yours. Please, please, peruse this very engaging, very important book from my friends Jimmy Dodd and Larry Magnuson. If you read it, it will help you understand your pastors and ministry leaders and what they go through every single day; if you take their words to heart, it will enable you to protect your shepherds' best interests, protract their ministry tenures, and produce even healthier and more active flocks."

John Ashmen, president of Association
of Gospel Rescue Missions

"This book is a must read for pastors and church leaders. Very few know the pressures a pastor and his family face, but Larry Magnuson goes below the surface understanding to address the pressures facing ministry families. Out of his two decades of support of ministry couples through SonScape Retreats, he speaks from a deep well of experience and compassion for pastors."

Dr. Michael Lewis, executive director
of pastoral care and development for
North American Mission Board

"This book offers tools to help the pastor, the pastor's family, and the people they serve to better understand and appreciate the roles of each. *Pastors Are People Too* is a call for those of us who name the name of Christ to help each other embrace our mandate to make the church the light that offers hope in our ever-darkening world."

Verdell Davis Krisher, SonScape Ministries
board member and author of *Let Me
Grieve, but Not Forever* and *Someday When
I Am Old, by a Not Yet Old Mom*

"The pastors in our churches are often struggling to thrive, not because they aren't loved, but because few of us in the church family understand the unique needs pastors have in their service to those they oversee. Jimmy Dodd and Larry Magnuson have had unprecedented access to the inner lives of pastors struggling to find their footing forward. Preventative steps by elder boards and congregants can lead to healthier pastors and, in turn, healthier church bodies. *Pastors Are People Too* helps guide those in community around pastors to provide this support that can help both the pastor and the church family thrive."

Mark Matlock, president of Youth Specialties

"In their book *Pastors Are People Too*, authors Dodd and Magnuson capture both the challenges of pastoral ministry and ways that congregations and lay leaders can provide much-needed support and encouragement to those serving as pastors. As one whose role it is to work with pastors, lay leaders, and congregations, I look forward to utilizing this resource in the churches under my charge in order to help foster a better understanding of the pastoral role and both the blessings and the challenges associated with it. While the book is written primarily using the male vernacular [for grammatical simplicity], I would encourage church leaders to glean wisdom from its pages regardless of whether your pastor is a man or a woman. You will not be sorry you did!"

Rev. Mark R. Stromberg, superintendent
of the Northwest Conference of the
Evangelical Covenant Church

Jimmy Dodd | Larry Magnuson

Pastors
— Are —
People
Too

**What They Won't *Tell You* but You
*Need to Know***

— A —
PastorServe
— RESOURCE —

David C Cook®
transforming lives together

PASTORS ARE PEOPLE TOO
Published by David C Cook
4050 Lee Vance View
Colorado Springs, CO 80918 U.S.A.

David C Cook Distribution Canada
55 Woodslee Avenue, Paris, Ontario, Canada N3L 3E5

David C Cook U.K., Kingsway Communications
Eastbourne, East Sussex BN23 6NT, England

The graphic circle C logo is a registered trademark of David C Cook.

The website addresses recommended throughout this book are offered as a
resource to you. These websites are not intended in any way to be or imply an
endorsement on the part of David C Cook, nor do we vouch for their content.

Unless otherwise noted, all Scripture quotations are taken from the ESV® Bible
(The Holy Bible, English Standard Version®), copyright © 2001 by Crossway, a
publishing ministry of Good News Publishers. Used by permission. All rights
reserved. Scripture quotations marked NIV are taken from the Holy Bible, NEW
INTERNATIONAL VERSION®, NIV®. Copyright © 1973, 2011 by Biblica, Inc.®
Used by permission. All rights reserved worldwide. NEW INTERNATIONAL
VERSION® and NIV® are registered trademarks of Biblica, Inc. Use of either
trademark for the offering of goods or services requires the prior written consent
of Biblica, Inc.; NLT are taken from the Holy Bible, New Living Translation,
copyright © 1996, 2007 by Tyndale House Foundation. Used by permission of
Tyndale House Publishers, Inc., Carol Stream, Illinois 60188. All rights reserved;
and THE MESSAGE are taken from THE MESSAGE. Copyright © by Eugene
H. Peterson 1993, 2002. Used by permission of Tyndale House Publishers,
Inc. The author has added italics to Scripture quotations for emphasis.

LCCN 2015952966
ISBN 978-1-4347-0921-9
eISBN 978-1-4347-1009-3

© 2016 Jimmy Dodd and Larry Magnuson
Published in association with the literary agency of Wolgemuth & Associates, Inc.
The Team: Alex Field, Jamie Chavez, Nick Lee, Jack Campbell, Susan Murdock
Cover Design: Amy Konyndyk
Printed in the United States of America
First Edition 2016
1 2 3 4 5 6 7 8 9 10

022616

Jimmy:

To Sally. My wife and best friend. You have lovingly journeyed with me, faithfully believed in me, consistently inspired me, and gently motivated me throughout our marriage. Your devotion to the Lord Jesus and the truth of the gospel is a daily encouragement to me. This book is as much yours as it is mine.

Larry:

To Barbara, the love of my life! You have taught me much about intimacy in marriage and in relationship with God. Through all the years of ministry you have been at my side—what an adventure we have had!

CONTENTS

Foreword

Charles Haddon Spurgeon, the great Baptist "prince of preachers," once told his students that if they could be happy doing something besides being a pastor, they should do it. Why? Because the Bible says God holds teachers *of* the Bible to a very high standard. There is a second reason behind Spurgeon's counsel: *being a pastor is hard.*

One day in my midtwenties, while studying to become a pastor, I came across a suicide note published in the local newspaper. The note was from a pastor.

> God forgive me for not being any stronger than I am. But when a minister becomes clinically depressed, there are very few places where he can turn to for help … It feels as if I'm sinking farther and farther into a downward spiral of depression. I feel like a drowning man, trying frantically to lift up my head to take just one more breath. But one way or another, I know I am going down.

The writer was the promising young pastor—still in his thirties—of a large, thriving church in St. Louis, Missouri. Having secretly battled depression for a long time, and having sought help through prayer, therapy, and medication, he did not have the will to claw through yet another day. In his darkest hour, the pastor decided he would rather join the angels than continue facing demons for years to come.

Some of those "demons," it turned out, were high-powered members of his church, whose expectations of him were impossibly high.

Not many months after this, another pastor, also from St. Louis, asphyxiated himself because of a similar secret depression.

The news of these two pastor suicides rocked my world. How could these men—both gifted pastors who believed in Jesus, preached grace, and comforted others with gospel hope—end up *losing hope* for themselves?

As the stories of these pastors became more public, it turned out that both of them shared an all-too-common reality for pastors. Both were surrounded by large crowds and yet felt alone in the world, *especially* in their churches. Each pastor had plenty of adoring fans, but neither felt that he had actual friends.

In his suicide note, the first pastor said he felt trapped. He was isolated and depressed but did not feel he could let this be known because it would ruin his ministry. Pastors, he had come to believe, weren't allowed to be weak. Pastors, he had come to believe, were not allowed to be human like everybody else.

Unfortunately, the feelings of those two pastors from St. Louis are not rare. Many of us pastors, including Spurgeon and including me, have fallen into the emotional abyss—not in spite of the fact that we are in ministry, but *because* we are in ministry.

Studies show that pastors experience anxiety and depression at a rate that is disproportionately high compared to the rest of the population. Because of the unique pressures associated with spiritual warfare, unrealistic expectations from congregants and oneself, the

freedom many feel to criticize and gossip about pastors with virtu-
ally zero accountability (especially in the digital age), failure to take
time off for rest and replenishment, marriage and family tensions
as a result of the demands of ministry, financial strains, and self-
comparison, pastors are prime candidates for emotional collapse.

Studies also show that some pastors face unreasonable, even
impossible, demands placed on them by their people. Dr. Thom
Rainer, a leading pastoral ministry guru, once conducted a survey
asking church members what they expected from their pastors.
Specifically, Dr. Rainer wanted to know the *minimum* amount of
time church members believed their pastors should give each week to
various areas of ministry, including prayer, sermon preparation, outreach and evangelism, counseling, administrative tasks, visiting the
sick, community involvement, denominational engagement, church
meetings, worship services, and so on. On average, the *minimum*
amount of time church members expected their pastors to give to the
ministry was 114 hours per week.[1]

Ministry can also take a toll on the pastor's family. When church
members don't like the pastor's sermon, when they don't like the
direction of the church, when they think the music is too loud (or too
soft), when they believe the pastor should wear a suit instead of jeans
(or jeans instead of a suit), when the pastor moves someone's cheese
or messes with their "sacred cow," the pastor's spouse can become a
sounding board for disgruntled and complaining members. Second
only to those who are married to public officials, no spouse in the
world is thrust into the line of "friendly fire" more than a pastor's
spouse. For this very reason, it took my wife forty-five minutes to say
yes to my marriage proposal! The pastor's spouse can also experience

loneliness, because in some churches, the pastor is expected to be as available to the church as he is to his own family.

Then there are the PKs—the "pastor's kids"—those little ones in the church who are expected by some to act like mature grown-ups. Both consciously and subconsciously, the pastor's kids feel that they are not allowed to be *kids* as their peers are. They feel a unique pressure to please, to perform, to play the part, to put on a show, and to be on their best behavior at all times. For some, this pressure leads to perfectionism and stress. For others, it leads to rebellion. It can be difficult for the pastor's kids to blend into the crowd and develop their own identities and personalities—because unlike most kids, they live their lives in the public eye. Being connected to the pastor fuels a lot of unspoken (and sometimes spoken) pressure for a six-year-old, or for a teenager, to navigate.

It is because of these unique realities of pastoral life that I am so grateful for Jimmy Dodd and Larry Magnuson. Jimmy was my first pastor-mentor out of seminary. He and his lovely wife, Sally, taught Patti and me, through the way that they lived their lives and the way that they treated us, that indeed pastors are people too. They welcomed us into their home, invited us into community with their children (and also with their dog, Shasta, who looked more like a reindeer than a dog), fed us repeatedly from their grill, took us to college basketball games, prayed for us and encouraged us, mentored us in ministry, and shared their lives with us. *For Jimmy and Sally, equipping and sending us out to plant our first church felt very SECONDARY to their commitment to love us.* We will never forget that.

Ever since that time in the late 1990s, our mentors from those first years have remained our cheerleaders and friends. The ministry to pastors that Jimmy has built, PastorServe, has become a magnificent extension of what Patti and I were privileged to experience in those early mentoring days.

Jimmy and Larry are not theorists about pastors and their congregations; they are among the best practitioners around. I represent hundreds, if not thousands, of pastors and churches that have gotten healthier and stronger because of these men and their ministry.

As for this book in particular, if you are a pastor (or pastor's spouse) in need of a good shot of encouragement—if you need to know that there's someone out there who *gets you*—I commend this wonderful book to you. Perhaps even more important, if you are a church member who wants to know how you can serve Jesus by supporting your pastor, this is without a doubt *the* book for you.

Scott Sauls,
senior pastor of Christ Presbyterian Church, Nashville,
author of *Jesus outside the Lines* and *BeFriend*

Why the State of Pastors Should Matter to You

George was stunned. His annual review was three sentences long and ended with the words "You will be replaced." Just a few months before, the congregation had stood in spontaneous applause honoring him for his leadership as pastor. Now the elders were firing him. They could not give him a reason other than a vague notion that new leadership was needed to take the church to the next level.

George is not alone. Thousands of pastors are fired every year. Others face waves of criticism that lead to discouragement and despair. Many would quit if they could find another way to support their families. The bottom line is, too many pastors are not at a good place, and given the chance, they would simply walk away.

It is a tragedy of epic proportion in the church today. Think that is an overstatement? We have both statistics and stories to back it up. The church in America is declining, and a major reason is the health of those called to lead.

This is a tragedy that affects you directly. You and your family depend on your pastor for spiritual guidance and the overall leadership of your church. If you want a dynamic church, living with biblical passion and making a difference in the world, you need a healthy pastor.

Jimmy and I have both worked for over twenty years in the local church. Across the last two decades, in our roles at PastorServe and

SonScape Retreats, we have listened to thousands of pastors share their deepest hurts and greatest hopes. This book is written to tell you what pastors often feel they cannot say themselves. We want to remove the facade and reveal the truth. The bottom line is, your pastor is struggling and desperately needs your help.

If you have no idea what your pastor is up against, but you want to understand, then this book is for you. If you want a healthy church and a healthy pastor, but you don't know what to do, then this book will give you tangible answers. If you want to see God-sized things happen in your church, but you aren't sure where to begin, you will find key steps in the pages that follow.

If you don't care, don't waste your time reading this book. But if you do care, and need help in knowing what to do, keep reading. By the time you finish, you will understand your pastor's world and how you can join him or her in making a difference in your church and your community.

Your Pastor's World

Several years ago I was told by leaders of a large denomination that one-third of their churches had fired a pastor in the last five years. While the statistics may vary between denominations, the problem spans them all. It is happening in small churches and large churches, rural and city churches, traditional and nontraditional churches.

Often it is a small group of disgruntled, influential people who begin a stir within the congregation. They focus on their pastor's weaknesses and faults; every pastor has some. If you look, you can always find places to criticize. But there is often a failure to balance pastors' shortcomings with their passions and strengths. Over time the voices of the few ring out above the words of the many. In most cases, when a pastor is fired or forced to resign, it is the result of a group of nine people or fewer, no matter what the size of the congregation. The few diminish their pastor while the majority of the church sits back and lets it happen.

The demands on pastors can be staggering. Pastors are asked to be dynamic preachers, compassionate counselors, capable administrators, bold visionaries, confident strategists, effective fund-raisers, strong leaders, and much more. The work is never done. Conflict comes from every side. Criticism is a common occurrence. Long hours suck life and energy. Fatigue and frustration set in. No one can live up to all the demands and remain healthy.

The intensity, the long hours, and the lack of understanding and appreciation by the people served often bring pastors to a place of despair. Most of the time they work through the thoughts and emotions, but not always. Sometimes they quit, most often leaving and feeling like failures.

Some have said as many as fifteen hundred pastors are quitting pastoral ministry every month. Whatever the actual number is, it is way too high. We are losing gifted, committed men and women. Losing so many of our pastors called to lead our churches is a tragedy with far-reaching effects.

What is happening is impacting the health and vitality of churches and pastors alike. In his bestselling book *The Emotionally Healthy Church*, Peter Scazzero writes: "The overall health of any church or ministry depends primarily on the emotional and spiritual health of the leadership."[1]

It's true. Your pastor's health should matter to you and to your church. And not just your pastor's health, but the health of the other pastors serving in your community and beyond. Worn-out, weary, depressed pastors are not able to help their churches live as light and salt in their communities. Until pastors and the people they serve understand how essential they are to each other, the church will struggle to accomplish its calling in the world.

Most pastors do not like to complain about the burdens they carry. They don't want to appear to their people as whiners. Let me try to paint you a picture of a day in the life of a pastor.

> **4:45 a.m.:** The alarm rings after what seems like only a few hours of sleep. You rise, take a quick shower, and head to a men's Bible study at a local restaurant.

> **5:30 a.m.:** Only three of the six men who said they were committed to the study show up, but there is still some good interaction and prayer among the three. One of the men is quieter than normal and asks to talk after the others have left. He breaks down in the parking lot. He has been terminated from his job. He doesn't know what to do. You try to encourage him, but words and even prayer seem empty as the man sobs before you.

> **7:30 a.m.:** Back in your office you know you should start working on your sermon, but instead you

check your email. After deleting the junk mail, you have twenty-three new emails that need a response. With the sixteen you never got to yesterday, that makes thirty-nine for today. You just finish the sixth response when your cell phone rings. There has been an accident involving one of your high schoolers. Her parents are distraught. You drop everything and head to the hospital.

9:30 a.m.: You arrive at the hospital and go into the ER. The parents are with their daughter. Everyone is pretty shook up, but aside from a few bruises and cuts, the girl will be okay. You take some time to pray with them and then slip away.

10:00 a.m.: Because you are at the hospital, you decide to stop and see Rachel. She is only eight years old and is suffering from a rare form of cancer. You enter the room and know the news is not good. Rachel's mom is sobbing. Her dad is talking with the doctor. Things are looking dim. By the time you leave, you are emotionally exhausted but cannot get Rachel and her parents off your mind.

12:45 p.m.: You arrive fifteen minutes late for a luncheon appointment. Tim and his family have been attending the church for a couple of years. You know almost immediately that they are leaving!

They've found a better youth program at another church. You do your best to be encouraging, but inside this is a big blow.

1:30 p.m.: You head back to church and the emails. You need to get to your sermon! There is a knock at the door. It is the janitor and the worship director. Conflict, again. These two can't seem to get along. In the end, they both leave mad.

3:00 p.m.: A couple comes in for marriage counseling. You married them just two years ago, but now the relationship is falling apart. For almost an hour you listen to them yell and blame. Your heart breaks, even as you try to help them see the truth. Maybe there is a little progress—maybe.

4:30 p.m.: You rush to your son's basketball game. Late as usual, but at least you got to see him play. You head home for dinner with the family. Your wife seems distant, probably upset at hours given to the church, but you don't have time to talk about it now.

6:30 p.m.: The elder board meeting is long, hard, and conflictive. It seems all the time is spent talking about insignificant things, and there is a lot of criticism.

9:30 p.m.: Before heading home, you stop by your office. There is a letter on your desk from a young man who has been attending the church for a few weeks. His life has been a disaster. He just wanted to say thanks for the sermons and to let you know he made a commitment to Jesus last Sunday. *Wow!* All the pain and frustration of the day dim as you read and reread the letter. "Thank You, Lord. I needed that!" You realize how tired you are and you have another breakfast meeting tomorrow morning. "Lord, forgive me for where I have failed today and help me do better tomorrow."

Not every day in a pastor's life is as intense as what you have just read, but many of them are. I also realize that other men and women engage in careers that demand long hours and incredible energy—law enforcement, firefighters, emergency room personnel, to name just a few. You may be saying to yourself, "Wait a minute, I work long hours to care for my family. Why should I be concerned about my pastor's schedule?"

Pastors are no different than anyone else in the church. No better, no worse. But they are called to wrestle with spiritual issues on a daily basis and to help you and your church family to dig deeper into the Word of God. Each week pastors are called to open God's Word to interpret and apply its truth for the people who listen. Any pastor for whom that fact does not bring a sense of inadequacy, or even "fear and trembling," ought to consider more deeply what he does. It is no small thing to stand before people with the Bible in hand to teach and preach God's truth week after week.

But the pastor's role involves much more than the Sunday sermon. Each week pastors are asked to bring godly counsel, hope, wisdom, and help into people's lives. Pastors engage with people in the midst of crisis as well as in times of joy. They stoop to answer the questions of a child, and they bring comfort to the elderly. The days of a pastor are planned, but always with enough flexibility for the unexpected.

While pastors are to be spiritual leaders, they also manage a business with an annual budget of hundreds of thousands of dollars, if not more. Some are fortunate enough to have paid staff, but most of the time they work with volunteers—volunteers who have strong opinions about how the church should operate and how the pastor should be spending his time. It has been said that 85 percent of a pastor's job involves managing complex relationships and business operations. I guarantee you that most pastors feel very inadequate and undertrained in those areas.

Then there are people's expectations. Expectations that come from all directions—denominational leaders, colleagues, church leaders, laypeople, family, and self. Too often the needs and expectations carried by pastors are crushing the life out of them.

As the weight grows on the pastor's shoulders, more often than not, the first thing neglected is his own personal spiritual life, followed closely by the pastor's time with his family. Bible study and time in prayer are essential parts of the pastor's responsibility, but the tyranny of the urgent pushes the imperatives into the background. A sense of futility grips the heart. Doubt and even depression begin to set in.

The day eventually comes when every person who attends a church is faced by crisis: death of a family member, a wayward child, a life-changing accident or illness, a marriage in trouble, loss of a job. What they need is a pastor whose emotional and spiritual condition is healthy and ready to speak to their need.

I was the youth pastor at a church when all the pastors were called and told one of our church members had dropped dead of a massive heart attack while playing softball. Bill was a young man. I will never forget meeting his wife and their two young boys as they walked into the emergency room; their faces white as they saw us. Delivering the news that Bill was gone left an indelible impact on me. How desperately they needed their pastors at that moment.

Destined to Fail without Help!

Our world needs Jesus. It needs the church to be alive and vibrant. The local church you attend needs the same. That will happen only when your pastors and laypeople work together for the sake of God's kingdom. Pastors will fail in their role and their calling without the help of their people—without you!

Even Jesus sought help. Only hours from the cross, He walked with His disciples toward the Garden of Gethsemane, fully aware of what lay ahead. In that moment, even the Son of God looked for help from those He trusted. Entering the garden, He asked three of the disciples He leaned on most to stand with Him—to pray with Him and for Him. Not once, but three times Jesus asked them to be by His side. Each time they were too tired and they fell asleep. Scripture records His painful cry: "So, could you not watch with me one hour?" (Matthew 26:40).

The burdens pastors carry cannot be compared to Jesus at the cross, but like Him, pastors often feel they are carrying their burdens alone! Far too many times pastoral couples have sat with Barbara and me at our retreat center with tears running down their faces, saying, "If only we had even one person, one couple that understood and cared." One! Just one!

I believe that in every church there is one person, one couple that cares. In fact, I am convinced there are several, if not many. But somehow understanding and communication have broken down … or life has gotten too busy … or pastors don't share what is really going on inside, and people don't ask. Whatever the reason, this pattern has to be reversed or pastors will fail in their responsibilities and calling. That failure will affect you and those you love.

You can be the one person. You can be the couple that stands and prays with your pastor. The difference can be you.

Remember the story of Moses holding his staff high in the air while the Israelites faced their first adversary on the way from Egypt to the Promised Land? The Amalekites threatened their very lives, while Joshua led an army of bricklayer slaves into battle. Moses stood at the top of a hill with Aaron and Hur at his side. As long as Moses held high the staff, the staff God had given him at his calling, the Israelites were victorious. But the battle dragged on and Moses's arms grew weary and began to drop. When the staff lowered, the Amalekites pushed back. The Israelites were in jeopardy because Moses was growing weak and weary. Then Aaron and Hur stepped forward. They found a rock for Moses to sit on, and each grabbed one of Moses's arms and lifted high the staff until the victory was won (Exodus 17:8–16).

Who played the crucial role in accomplishing God's plan—Moses, Joshua, the army, or Aaron and Hur? The truth is they all were needed! The same is true for the church today—pastor, lay leader, church member—all are needed!

There are too many stories of pastors who falter under the weight they carry because no one steps in to lend a hand. But there are other stories; stories in which the people of a church stand with their pastor, sharing the burden of ministry. Let me share two of those stories. One is the story of Jerry and Nancy Walsh; the other is my own.

Jerry pastors a growing congregation near Orlando, Florida. He and his wife, Nancy, have become good friends of mine and have given me permission to tell and quote their story prior to the release of their book. High school sweethearts, Jerry and Nancy got married and, not long afterward, planted the church. Everything looked wonderful, at least on the outside. But Nancy hadn't dealt with some deep wounds from her past.

The wounds erupted into sinful behavior that not even Nancy understood. In their as-yet-unpublished book, *A Reason to Hope*, they tell the story of Nancy's affair, Jerry's faithful pursuit, and God's amazing redemption. Nancy describes her journey with openness and brutal honesty, giving the most powerful look inside the heart and mind of a prodigal that I have ever read.

God did an extraordinary work of redemption, bringing Nancy back to Himself, to Jerry, and to their children. The day after Nancy returned, Jerry went to meet with his elders, ready to resign his position as senior pastor:

> We met in Phill's (one of the elders) living room. I explained the situation and told them that we would be moving away. It was at this moment that God used Phill to change the whole equation of our tenure at our church. "You are not going to make this decision just twenty-four hours after the most emotional day of your life," he counseled. The others agreed. They asked me to take ninety days off and focus on marriage reconciliation and what God wanted us to do next. I told them I would take the time, but I was sure we would be moving. I did not see any way we could stay. Looking back, I am so grateful for these wise elders and their advice, support, prayers, and even their admonishment at times.

Nancy wanted to leave—to run.

> When you have done some of the most awful things you can imagine ... when you have embarrassed yourself beyond belief ... when you have messed up royally, the last thing you want to do is face it. The impulse is to run. The idea of leaving the area, of packing up our family and saying good-bye to our church for good, was all very appealing to me.

My preference would have been to run. I was used to running. I'd been running my whole life. But my running days were over! I told Jerry, "Do not spare me from the consequences of what I have done."

Together Nancy and Jerry went on, what they now call, the "Apology Tour." Nancy asked God to give her the names of the people she needed to sit with face to face and ask their forgiveness. The list was long! It included standing before the congregation and asking them to forgive her. Nancy says:

> The truth is most churches do not know what to do with sin … "big" sin, at least. Our church chose to handle my affair differently. Things were dealt with, not only publicly, but with overflowing Christ-like grace. Forgiveness and reconciliation became a reality. Our church members do not know how extraordinary they are. They did not turn a blind eye, or run away, or attack the sinner. They loved and forgave me like Jesus did, and together we were able to experience what few churches ever know.[2]

It has been over eight years since Nancy came home—home to Jesus, to her family, and to her church. Jerry is still the pastor, and while some chose to leave for a variety of reasons, most stayed. The church has grown—in numbers certainly—but even more, the church has grown in its understanding of what it means to be the church of Jesus Christ. Barbara and I watched firsthand as the church leaders and the church members struggled with what to do during those turbulent months. The faithfulness and courage of all involved turned a tragedy into a beautiful story of redemption.

My Story

I know what it means to hurt as a person and as a pastor. I spent two decades serving the local church and the prior twenty years growing up in a pastor's home.

It was in the spring of 1989 when my world was shattered. My dad was removed from ministry for moral failure. It became a huge story in Minneapolis, appearing in local papers, on television, and even in *USA Today*. Lives were damaged, lawsuits filed, my dad went to jail, and the church he had served (and where I had grown up) was devastated. As always, there is a story behind the story, but let me simply say, for me, it was a time of exceptional pain and doubt.

Barbara and I had just launched a new church plant in a northern suburb of Minneapolis. I will never forget the Sunday I stood before our little congregation, meeting in a local elementary school, to give an explanation for what they were hearing on the local news.

The words I shared are long forgotten, but I remember vividly what happened. Partway through my attempt to explain the *what* and the *why*—I broke down! Standing before that group of people, filled with my own doubts, fears, and questions, I began to weep!

There, amid my sobs and gasps for breath, something happened that changed the course of my life. A man by the name of Tom Lundberg got up from his chair, walked up on the platform, and put his arm around me. He came to stand beside me, and then others came. It was the moment that saved my ministry. I was not alone.

More than what it did for me, it became a picture of who we were going to be as a church. From that day on we became a people committed to loving and caring for others. We did not do it perfectly. There were many failures along our journey. Yet we became known in our community as a place where people could go with their wounds and find acceptance. It was a church with an imperfect pastor and a broken people waiting with open arms for anyone to come join our family.

Standing with Pastors

Fifteen years ago, God called Barbara and me to another ministry that came alongside us in our crisis—a place called SonScape Retreats. For the last decade and a half, it has been our privilege to put our arms around broken, wounded pastors, missionaries, and parachurch leaders, letting them know they are not alone nor forgotten. Some just need a safe place to come away for rest and renewal. Others are beat up, burned out, and losing hope. But the one thing they all have in common is the need for someone to encourage them, to stand with them, to be the church for them. For more than thirty years, SonScape Retreats has been a place where Christian leaders can come for comfort and guidance, and for the healing process to begin.

As important as it is for pastors to come away from time to time to a place provided for them, what is more essential is help in the trenches and on the front lines of ministry. They need people like you who understand they are broken, imperfect people just like everyone else. They need people willing to roll up their sleeves and join the work. Where there is a fellowship of like-minded companions, the journey becomes a joyful adventure.

There are many examples of churches that love and care for their pastors—and where pastors love and care for their churches. Places where people understand that their pastors will grow weary and that they will falter if they do not have Aarons and Hurs to come alongside them. Places where everyone knows burdens are to be shared by the many, not carried by the one.

The tragedy of wounded, broken, burned-out pastors can be overcome if all of us—pastor, church leaders, and church members—work together.

Our hope is that this book will be a field guide for those who want to understand, encourage, and come alongside the men and women called to lead the church. Jimmy and I fully recognize that sometimes the problems lie within the pastors themselves. Many books in this series will speak to those issues. This book addresses the need for people within the church to share the burden of ministry with those who lead. Each chapter will take on one issue and, in the end, offer practical steps that can be taken. *Together, and only together, we can turn tragedy into triumph!*

Chapter 1

Your Pastor Needs a Champion
It Could Be You

Luke is a pastor of a growing, thriving church in New England. He and his wife planted the church fifteen years ago—and the Lord has blessed them. The church has grown to nearly two thousand in attendance. The church just completed their second building campaign, which added a much-needed permanent worship space, allowing the church to move from three services back to two and thus easing the stress on Luke, the worship team, the nursery, and generally everybody! The staff is healthy, the leadership team is comprised of godly leaders who are much more than smart business leaders, and the gospel is preached. All is right with the world, right?

While year fifteen is cause for celebration, the road to their present location has been filled with obstacles, detours, and heartache. Luke has led through the difficult days with grace and zeal, which I have seen in few pastors.

Several months ago Luke came to me in a state of exhaustion. He was discouraged, fatigued, and considering leaving the church to which he and his wife had given their lives. In many ways, Luke's state of despair made little sense. Many pastors would love to lead a church family with the staff, leadership, and facility of

this growing church. Yet, here sat Luke, ready to walk away from
it all.

After several hours of talking through Luke's discouragement,
we came to the care that Luke himself was receiving. "Honestly,"
Luke said, "I feel as if I go to great lengths to champion my staff. I
regularly go to bat for the staff with our elders. I work to get them
a generous salary, a healthy benefits package, opportunity for rest,
and opportunities for continuing education. I work hard to create
a grace-centered environment where everyone is free to take risks
and everyone is free to fail. I recently heard someone in the church
complaining about our children's pastor's work ethic, and I ardently
went to her defense, passionately explaining to the person that they
have no idea the work going on behind the scenes that no one will
ever see. I regularly affirm my staff in front of the congregation. The
staff knows with 100 percent certainty that I have their back. All of
that is good and right as I believe that a key role I play as lead pastor
is to zealously champion my staff. And yet, my heart is discouraged
to the point of quitting. The problem is simply this: I don't have
anyone championing me."

Luke is not alone in his observation. In church after church, I
meet with lead pastors who do not feel as if they have a champion.
They lack that one person who has made it a personal goal to watch
out for them. In Luke's case, in year three of the church, a financial shortfall nearly caused them to close the doors. Luke reduced
his salary by 50 percent, sold multiple personal assets (including
his car), and dipped into retirement savings to make payroll—for
three months! In other words, Luke gave it all. Yet, when the church
reached a place of financial health (in year seven), the sacrifice that

Luke and his family had made was all but forgotten. But still, Luke and his family worked to dig out of their deep financial hole, the result of extreme generosity on the part of Luke and his wife. In year ten (seven years after the financial crisis), Luke's salary had yet to be restored to the level it had been in year three when he voluntarily took the reduction.

The failure to correct Luke's situation was not an intentional slight. People were not ungrateful for the incredible leadership Luke provided the congregation. If the church had any clue of the financial burden the family was bearing, they would have immediately come to their aid. The problem was the same problem that plagues thousands of congregations when it comes to the care of their pastors. People simply forgot.

The Power of Remembering

Perhaps it's the world's greatest excuse—I forgot. I didn't get you a gift for our anniversary because I forgot our anniversary. I wasn't slighting you when I missed our date; I simply forgot. Nothing passive aggressive here; I simply forgot to pick you up at the airport. I can relate.

I forget where I put my keys, my sunglasses, and my phone. I forget names, birthdates, and anniversaries (thankfully, never my own). I seldom forget promises because most are made to my children and they love to remind me of my promised commitments. Nearly every website has a place to go if you forget your user name or password. Why? Because people forget! Our minds are overloaded with information and we easily forget.

As followers of Jesus, we need to understand two basic truths: God remembers and we forget. Or, stated another way, God doesn't forget and we often fail to remember. Over and over again in Scripture we are reminded that God remembers. More than ten times we are told that God remembered His covenant promise to the nation of Israel. Psalm 105:8–11 says,

> He remembers his covenant forever,
>   the word that he commanded, for a thousand
>   generations,
> the covenant that he made with Abraham,
>   his sworn promise to Isaac,
> which he confirmed to Jacob as a statute,
>   to Israel as an everlasting covenant,
> saying, "To you I will give the land of Canaan
>   as your portion for an inheritance."

Our heavenly Father remembers His children. He remembered Noah (Genesis 8:1; 9:14–16), Abraham (Genesis 19:29; Psalm 105:42), and Isaac and Jacob (Exodus 2:23–25; Leviticus 26:42). God remembered Rachel (Genesis 30:22) and Hannah (1 Samuel 1:19–20), allowing them to conceive. We are told that God remembers the afflicted (Psalm 9:12). Just as powerful are the times when God chooses not to remember. Jeremiah 31:33–34 reminds us that God chooses to remember our sin no more.

The Scriptures encourage believers over and over again to remember. In Jonah 2:7, we read that at his lowest point, when he thought that all was lost, Jonah remembered the Lord. In Luke

17:11–19, Jesus healed ten lepers, and yet only one remembered to return to give thanks. Unquestionably, all were immensely grateful, yet only one expressed gratitude. We need the Holy Spirit because, apart from His work, we would forget the words of Jesus (John 14:26). Perhaps the supreme command for believers to remember came from the lips of Jesus at the Last Supper when He said to celebrate the Lord's Supper remembering Him (Luke 22:19; 1 Corinthians 11:24).

Luke's Story Continues

There was more to Luke's story though. "I felt like I would be viewed as an ungrateful, bitter jerk if I were to bring this up to the elders. Year after year I fought for the staff before the elders with the realization that no one was fighting for me. One year, after the staff had all gone the extra mile during our first building campaign, I asked the elders to consider giving the staff a year-end bonus to thank them for their prolonged service and sacrifice. The elders loved the idea and gave the entire staff a generous year-end financial gift. Everyone that is except me. I kept waiting for one of the elders to say, 'Wait a minute—we can't do this for the entire staff and not do this for Luke!' But those longed-for words never came. While I could feel bitterness growing within my spirit, I couldn't bring myself to ask for myself what the elders were doing for others. In reality, if the elders had any idea how I felt, they would immediately make up my retirement (which had now been depleted for ten years), restore my salary, and apologize profusely. Yet, it just feels wrong for me to ask. I am reduced to praying that the Lord would give me a champion.

One person, just one person in leadership who would make it their mission to look out for me."

Do the words of Luke strike you as self-serving or narcissistic? You may be surprised to learn that I found Luke to be characterized by grace, love, sacrifice, kindness, and care. Luke's actions over the past several years had clearly demonstrated that he was anything but an egocentric leader. Luke was absolutely right. The simple fact was that he didn't have a champion.

Don't Mess with My Pastor

I had just spoken to a California church and was now meeting with a number of leaders in the church. We went around the room, each person introducing himself or herself and sharing the person's primary responsibility in the church. One young woman stood up and said, "My name is Carol and I work with the youth ministry." A middle-age man told me that he was the head of the hospitality team. Weston told me that he served as a part of the story team, using the church website to share people's stories with a broad audience. Around the room we went. Near the end, Edward, a tall, distinguished-looking, gray-haired gentleman who I would have guessed to be in his late seventies, stood up. With great passion he announced, "I'll tell you what my job is in this church. If anyone messes with my pastor, I'll kill 'em." *I love that!* I walked over and gave Edward a bear hug. May his tribe increase! To be clear, I doubt Edward would have really killed someone. But his passion to care for his pastor came through loud and clear. Edward went on to explain that if anyone was going to attack the pastor, they were going to need to go through him. He was vehemently devoted to his pastor.

Following the meeting, I approached Edward to learn more of his story. He explained that while he had spent his life in the insurance business, his father had been a pastor. He explained, "Time and time again, I saw my father come home late at night, emotionally beat up by the church board. Following church meetings, he would regularly come through the door with tears in his eyes. My mother would embrace him and then, every single time I can remember, my father and mother would sit on the couch and pray for each member of the board. They would pray for their marriages, their families, their health, and their businesses. Not once in all those years did I ever hear my father bad-mouth his board or talk them down. When my mother would tearfully refer to them as uncaring men, my father would gently calm her down, reminding her that they too were facing struggles of their own." Edward went on to tell me that he remembered his family enduring intense financial struggles. He recalled many nights his family had precious little food to eat, only to learn from board members' children the next day at school that they were dining in the nicest of restaurants. When I asked about family vacations, he cheerfully recalled a number of family vacations—all of which involved accompanying his father to a camp where he was the speaker. When I inquired about vacations where his father was 100 percent focused on the family, Edward couldn't recall a single one. And as a result, he vowed long ago that he would not let that happen to whoever would serve his family in the role of pastor. This wasn't blind loyalty. Edward assured me he knew of many of his pastor's faults. And yet, he remained steadfastly committed to guarding his pastor's back. He was championing his pastor.

Edward's story is unusual. It is unusual because the story usually has a tragic end. In my years of caring for pastors, their spouses, and their families, I am most grieved when I hear stories of pastors' children who determine that they will never have anything to do with the church for the rest of their lives because of how they saw the church treat their parents. Unlike Edward, who stayed in the church determined to meet a glaring omission, many simply walk away, embittered, vowing to never again step foot into a church.

Everyone Needs Affirmation

Because I have five children, I have spent more time at back-to-school night than the average parent. Each of these nights includes a visit to my child's classroom (my wife and I divide and conquer) to hear from the teacher and parent volunteer classroom coordinator. The parent volunteer talks about drivers for field trips, who will host the Thanksgiving Feast, and teacher appreciation. At my children's school, teacher appreciation is a big deal—and rightly so. This is the person who will be spending a considerable amount of time with my child over the next nine months. I want him or her to feel special. The parent volunteer explains that, each month, two families will have the task of specifically encouraging the teacher. A list is commonly provided that lists the teacher's favorite cookie, candy, ice cream, pizza, color, song, author, Starbucks drink, and many more. The list is to allow the designated encouragers to have some direction if they want to drop off a note with a plate of cookies or a book from the teacher's favorite author. This is no secret. The teacher is commonly in the classroom as the announcement is made. At our school, this is just standard operating procedure. And you know what? I like it! Why not encourage the ones who will day by day pour heart and soul into my children?

Similarly, at the close of every sports season, a designated parent will ask for five or ten dollars from every parent to say thanks to the coach for volunteering his or her time. I gladly contribute. There are organized efforts to say thank you to music teachers, dance teachers, and art teachers. One of my daughters participated for a number of years in gymnastics. The coach's thank-you gift—a hefty cash bonus—was added directly to your bill! There was no option! You were going to express thanks to the coach—or your daughter would no longer be on the gymnastics team! I could go on and on.

Here is where this becomes perplexing. Why do we appropriately go to such great lengths to express thanks to those who pour into our lives, and yet, the ones who may pour into our lives more than anyone else, our pastors, commonly go a lifetime without being thanked with anything other than a verbal thank-you? I'm not pushing for a "gymnastics coach" cash gift. I'm pushing for a handwritten note saying how much you appreciate your pastor's care. I'm advocating for you to go out of your way to defend your pastor if you hear someone gossiping behind his back. And then—verbally express your love and affirmation to your pastor.

You might be surprised to learn that I am not a huge fan of October being designated "Pastor Appreciation Month." I'm guessing this annual "holiday" was invented by a greeting card company as a way to sell cards. I believe that every day of every month is an appropriate time for pastor appreciation (just like at the close of Mother's Day, we remind our children that in the Dodd household, every day is Mother's Day). I have heard people in the church say ludicrous things such as, "I was going to do something special for our pastor, but I missed Pastor Appreciation Month, so I'll just wait until next October." *Every month is pastor appreciation month!* Don't wait to express gratitude to your pastor.

Everyone Needs a Champion

Everyone needs to know that there is someone cheering him on in the race of life. I was privileged to grow up in a home in which my parents' presence at my sporting events was one of their highest priorities in life. I honestly can't remember my father missing a basketball game, football game, swim meet, or track meet (clearly, this was in the day when children were not required to specialize in a sport, forsaking all others by age four). I know he never missed a baseball game because he was the coach of my team from the time I was a small child. It always meant the world to me to know that someone was in the stands, cheering for me. Knowing that someone is cheering for you makes anyone perform at a higher level.

There are numerous studies detailing the impact of home field advantage. Simply stated, it is well documented that the home team always wins more games than the visiting team. This is true in all four professional American sports leagues (MLB, NHL, NBA, and NFL). The same is true for sports around the world. In fact, the two sports with the highest home win percentage are European soccer and NBA basketball, both exceeding 60 percent. The host country of the Olympics always performs at a higher level than in years in which they travel to another country. Why do teams play better at home? While theories abound, the general consensus is that individuals and teams perform at a higher level when the majority of fans are cheering for them. We all want to know that there are those who are *for* us.

Speaking from a purely objective, unbiased perspective, I believe my wife, Sally, is the world's greatest teacher. She has a gifting with children that I consider to be purely God given. Children love Sally, and they consistently perform at high levels when she is their teacher. If she tutors a child facing special challenges, the child will regularly make incredible progress while under her tutelage. Why? Because even young children can sense when someone is championing them. Sally's students know she is in their corner and she will do anything in her power to help them succeed. The fact that she will go out of her way to attend sporting events, recitals, and performances of all kinds communicates to the youngest minds that she is cheering for them.

Pastors need to know that there are people firmly in their corner. Pastors need to be assured that there are those who are consistently cheering for them.

Hebrews 12:1–2 assures us that our hope as believers is that Jesus Christ is cheering for us as we run the race of life: "Therefore, since we are surrounded by so great a cloud of witnesses, let us also lay aside every weight, and sin which clings so closely, and let us run with endurance the race that is set before us, looking to Jesus, the founder and perfecter of our faith, who for the joy that was set before him endured the cross, despising the shame, and is seated at the right hand of the throne of God."

I also like the New Living Translation's wording in verse 2, which says, "We do this by keeping our eyes on Jesus, the champion who initiates and perfects our faith."

The promise is that Jesus Christ is our great champion. Some pastors are in very difficult circumstances that have left them feeling as though they have to be the hero, the champion, and the savior. They need to hear the message of Hebrews 12:1–2. They are not the champion. When pastors grasp that Jesus is the supreme hero of our story, the pressure is taken off them and placed squarely onto the shoulders of Jesus. In Jesus there is a champion, a savior, and a hero. Pastors don't have to save themselves, their families, or their congregations; that is the job of Jesus. Every member of every church needs to consistently hear the message that only Jesus is the hope of every church. Stated another way, your pastor is not the hope of your congregation. Similarly, the hope of the Democratic and Republican parties is not better leaders; their hope is Jesus. The hope of every fan of your favorite local sports team is not an all-star to lead the team to victory; their hope is Jesus. The hope of every person who sits in the congregation, and lives a broken life, is only Jesus.

The truths contained within Hebrews 12:1–2 should also give every believer hope. We are the "home team." We are surrounded by a massive crowd of fanatical saints, many of whom are referenced in Hebrews 11, who have run the race before us and are now gathered together to collectively cheer us on. They are assuring those still running the race, "By faith I have run and finished the race and I know that you can too" (my paraphrase).

Not long ago my wife and my daughter Megan ran a half marathon, their first. My daughters Paige, Allie, and Sarah and I stood alongside the race route as Sally and Megan ran. We had the route mapped out, and we arranged four spots along the route where we could cheer them on as they ran by. I was amazed at the size of the crowd, who were not just cheering on their loved ones, but everyone was cheering on all the runners! There were no detractors in the crowd. It was a beautiful experience as everyone was totally supportive. The crowd, which numbered in the thousands, held signs, gave high fives, rang cow bells, and shouted words of support and encouragement to runners they had never met. The most amazing thing took place as we stood close to the finish line to cheer on our family for the final time. I noticed that runners who had finished the race began making their way back to a location a couple of hundred yards from the finish line to look for and cheer on loved ones still running the race. They had finished the race, and they were now cheering on others with words echoing Hebrews 12:1–2. "Come on; you can do it! If I can do it, you can do it! You are so close; the finish line is just ahead." No one is going to quit the race when the finish line is in sight and your loved ones, who have already finished the race, are screaming words of encouragement as you take your final steps.

Every pastor needs to know he is surrounded by a congregation that is cheering him on.

Every Pastor Needs a Champion

It is the job of the lead pastor together with the board of elders (or designated leadership team) to champion the church staff. They should look for every opportunity to publicly affirm their team, thank their team, and praise their team. But it is solely the job of the board to champion the lead pastor. This won't happen by accident. The leadership is going to need to designate one or two leaders to have regular conversations with the pastor. If you are part of a church that is staff led and there is no overseeing board, a special pastoral care board needs to be established immediately. The following questions need to be asked a minimum of once a month. The questions are lengthy and are in no way intended to burden the pastor. While some may appear invasive, they are intended to reveal areas of life and ministry in which the pastor needs championing:

- What are you presently celebrating in Jesus Christ?
- How have you practically made your family your primary ministry and the church your secondary ministry over this past month?
- How has it been in your marriage? Are you taking the time to share your stories with each other? What are the conflicts you are facing together as a couple?
- What conflicts in the church are impacting your ministry? Are there any relational triangles that need to be collapsed?
- Are you presently living in a crisis mode? If yes, how long have you been in that crisis mode? What are the important areas of your life that are being shortchanged by crisis-mode living?

What do you need to say no to in order to allow the crisis mode to slowly disappear?

- How can you build more replenishing relationships into your life?
- What are the financial challenges that you are presently facing?
- What ministry expenses did you incur this past month that were not reimbursed?
- What debt did you incur in this last month? What was the reason for the debt?
- What do we need to know as elders that we don't presently know?
- How can I be praying for you and your family over this next month?
- What do your gauges on your "dashboard of life" read?

Emotional Energy

E_____1/4_____1/2_____3/4_____F

Physical Energy

E_____1/4_____1/2_____3/4_____F

Spiritual Life

E_____1/4_____1/2_____3/4_____F

One More Time—Back to Luke

I am happy to report that Luke courageously stepped up and disclosed his challenges to one elder. As you would imagine, the elder was embarrassed, bordering on humiliation for overlooking Luke's needs. After sharing Luke's situation with the remainder of the board, Luke was returned to pre-crisis-level salary. His board came to understand a small percentage of what Luke had sacrificed (although I doubt they will ever know the whole story of their pastor's sacrificial commitment to their church).

Thankfully, an elder has committed to serving as Luke's champion. He meets regularly with Luke, inquiring about the church, his family, his finances, and his emotional well-being. Just knowing that someone has his back has made an enormous difference in how Luke leads the church.

Remember, pastors will not champion themselves. Every pastor needs a champion. They need a team of two or three in the congregation in positions of leadership and authority who will champion regularly the needs of their pastor.

Chapter 2

Twenty-Four-Hour Pastor
Allow Your Pastor to Be a Real Person

"I don't want to be here, and I'm not going to share anything!" Scott and his wife, Diane, sat around the fireplace with three other couples the first night of their retreat. Arms crossed in a defiant posture, Scott made it clear he was not happy to be there.

"My elders sent us, but we don't need a pastor's retreat!" Scott and Diane had been in a bad place several months before, but things had improved, so in their minds (at least in Scott's) there was no reason for them to give up a week of time for a retreat.

Having left home at the age of fourteen, Scott pursued the life he wanted—the life of a cowboy. Scott lived his dream—herding cattle on the plains and in the mountains of Wyoming and Colorado. In time he married, but his relationship with Diane had been rocky from the beginning. Seeking help, Diane went to a marriage counselor. During one of the counseling sessions, Diane accepted Jesus as her Savior. Scott was furious. His father was a pastor, and Scott wanted nothing to do with faith or the church.

God had other plans. God pursued Scott, and Scott became not only a Christian but a pastor as well. Scott had a powerful presence about him. God used that strength and Scott's gift of preaching to bring many to Jesus. There was profound growth at the church.

Trouble was, Scott had no idea how or when to stop. Rest was not in his vocabulary, and play was unthinkable. He still loved horses and cowboying, and there was no time for the frivolous.

The turbulence of his past led Scott to become a driven man, always trying to outrun deep-rooted feelings that he would never measure up. The same drivenness was turned toward ministry. Year after year the church grew larger, taking more of a toll on Scott and Diane. Scott was anxious and stressed, and many of his negative personality traits were rising to the surface; he was losing sight of the real Scott. All he knew to do was keep pressing on.

He never sat in an easy chair that had been bought just for him. How could he? What if someone from the church came and saw him resting? Or worse, sleeping? They would think him lazy, and all his life he had believed there were very few things worse than being lazy. So Scott just kept giving and doing—and slowly losing more of his real personality.

The 24-7 Pastor

I (Larry) have a brother-in-law who is a family doctor. He is good at what he does. But often people, including my wife, will come up to him with questions when he is not at the office.

"I have a nagging pain right here. What should I do?" "My child has a fever of 103; should I be worried?" "How often should I have my cholesterol checked?"

Todd has a standard reply: "Call your doctor!" In other words, "I am not a doctor right now. I'm just Todd." During his times away from the office, Todd bikes, canoes the boundary waters in northern

Minnesota, serves on boards at the church, spends time with my sister and their children, laughs, and plays. Truly being "off" when he is not at the office helps him to be a better doctor when he is "on" and at the office. Many pastors could learn something from my brother-in-law.

How many times at an extended family gathering is a pastor asked to pray before the food is served? As if only a pastor can pray. How often at a neighborhood party does someone come up and say, "Pastor, this is my friend and she has some questions about the Bible. Could you talk with her?" How about the chance meeting in a grocery store that becomes a discussion about the children's program? In time, even the pastor's spouse can come to feel as though she is married to a role rather than a person. Children can see their father more as pastor than dad.

No one is healthy working twenty-four hours a day, seven days a week. In fact, it is not possible. Unfortunately too many people place that burden on their pastors, and too many pastors accept it. Rest and play are essential elements to a healthy life and ministry! They remind us of who we are beyond what we do. Without rest and play, the pastor's role will overtake and consume all of life—hobbies, activities, family, friendships, dreams—everything. While this can be a hazard for all people, it seems to be a very common one for pastors!

When is a pastor not a pastor? Too often the answer is *never*!

For most of the years I was in church ministry, the title "pastor" was permanently attached to your first name—Pastor Tom, Pastor John, *Pastor Larry*. I cannot tell you how often I just wanted to be plain-old Larry—no title, no role—just Larry. I should have drawn better boundaries. But I was young and unaware of what was happening.

Fortunately things have changed in recent decades. Much of the time today, the title has been dropped from the name. But only the title. The role still attaches itself and becomes the identity.

When we left our church in Minnesota and were called to serve in Colorado, we felt many losses. Most of our extended family attended the church we had served. So many friends and relationships were left behind, no longer to be a part of our daily lives. But we were unprepared for the reality that one of the relationships we missed the most was with a couple in our neighborhood, Chuck and Teri Johnson. They did not attend our church, but another in our community. When we walked and talked with them, I was not Pastor Larry. We did not talk about issues in the church. In fact, most of the time we did not even talk about spiritual things. We just talked and laughed and enjoyed each other's company. It was wonderful and life giving, and we found ourselves longing for those times again.

Too often pastors do not have a Chuck and Teri. In fact, many of them have no relationships or friendships outside the church. They have to be "on" all the time. Again, that can result from an inability to set clear boundaries. But it can also grow out of the actions and expectations of church members and church leaders.

At every retreat we lead, couples are asked about their hobbies and what kinds of things they do for fun. So many look at Barbara and me in confused silence. "Can pastors really have hobbies and fun?" They not only can; they must!

A 24-7 mentality in either a pastor or in the church he serves will eventually lead to disaster. Your pastor needs regular time away from his role, in order to be healthy as a person, as well as a pastor.

Beware of the Mask

The title of pastor does not protect a person from the "stuff" of life. Pastors get discouraged, wounded, overwhelmed, lonely, tempted, and all the other things that afflict humankind. Because of their role and high visibility, too often people forget that in these things pastors are really no different than anyone else.

Recently Barbara lost her father after a long battle with Alzheimer's. While we were glad to see him released from this world and sent home to his heavenly Father, it has still been a time of pain and grief for Barbara and her family. One of our alumni wrote a note of condolence in which she said, "I never thought of you and Larry experiencing pain and loss." Let me assure you, we do! Our pastor does. And so does yours.

Pastors struggle with emotions such as anger, fear, anxiety, and little joy. Some have a deep sense of failure or carry resentment and distrust. Some are plagued by perfectionism, rejection, or a critical spirit.

When a pastor lives "the role" too long, he is in danger of losing the realness of being a human and often constructs a facade to help him stay in the role. It is a mask that portrays the lie that a pastor never hurts, has it all together, and can rise to any occasion. Keeping this mask in place day after day becomes destructive to the pastor himself, to the family, and to the church he serves.

Barbara and I sit with many men and women who live the role so well they seem to think of themselves above being broken. Without realizing it, their sense of need for a Savior, in every way, fades.

The apostle Paul was a pastor. Yet he was crystal clear about his own weaknesses and struggles. He refused to wear the mask. Hear him say: "Christ Jesus came into the world to save sinners, of whom I am the foremost" (1 Timothy 1:15).

As soon as pastors start believing "it can't happen to me"—whatever the "it" might be—they are treading on dangerous ground. As soon as the people of a church begin thinking "it" could never happen to their pastor, they are being deceived by the mask he is portraying. As a result, they may not be as ardent in praying a wall of God's protection around their leader.

There is a ridiculous, disastrous notion that pastors should not need to see a counselor. That is all about the facade. All of us need help sometimes. Pastors may need to work with someone on their marriage, on abandonment issues from their past, on anger, or on a host of other things that can steal health and life from a person. They, like any of us, need help sometimes. We all need to understand what is going on inside and why. Then we all need to bring these things to the feet of Jesus.

When Barbara and I came to SonScape, I knew we would be spending a lot of time talking with couples one on one. I asked a counselor friend of mine if he had any insights for me. Among the many things he shared was a piece of wisdom: "Along life's journey we all get stuck sometimes. Counseling helps us understand the what and why of what is happening. But never forget it is Jesus who brings the healing."

What do you want in your pastor? Do you want someone hiding behind a mask that suggests he is beyond the struggles that affect your life? Or do you want a real person who brings godly principles to bear as he wrestles with hard issues of life—a real person who leaves an honest trail for you to follow? You can help make your church a safe place for your pastor to be a real person, as well as for everyone else who walks through the doors.

The elders of the church we served in Minnesota regularly sent us to SonScape Retreats and other growth experiences. They did it for our sake and for theirs. "You have so much more passion and insight when you take your time away, Pastor!" It was because in those times of refreshment I would regain myself, not as a pastor, but as the person God created me to be! The mask would diminish and the truth would be revealed. What they called "passion and insight" was simply the real Larry honestly wrestling with life and faith.

Some Ways You Can Help

1. **Honor and affirm the boundaries and time away your pastor sets.** Make sure days off, vacation, continuing education time, and sabbaticals are taken. Let your pastor know you recognize the importance of these times for the pastor's personal health and ministry. Encourage your pastor to rest, play, and engage in times of self-discovery and growth.

2. **Accept that your pastor will need to talk with someone sometimes, and encourage him to do so.** If your pastor needs counseling, be it with a licensed therapist or at a place like SonScape Retreats, encourage him to go. If you ever hear another church member speaking negatively of your pastor because he needs counseling, bring positive affirmations to the pastor's courage to seek guidance. Help make the funds available if needed.

3. **Recognize your pastor will need time to grieve.** Pastors who have experienced significant loss or have invested much time

walking with people through crisis must learn how to grieve. This is important for them personally, and it becomes a model for the people they serve. Boards can help by giving a few extra days off during an intense time. Grieving is imperative for every person's health, including pastors.

Pastors: There Are No Two Alike

When you have sat with as many pastors as I have, one thing becomes crystal clear—they are all different. In fact, aside from a commitment to Jesus and their call to ministry, I cannot think of another trait common to them all.

At SonScape Retreats we use the Myers-Briggs Type Indicator to help pastors and their spouses answer the question "Do you know who you are?" The most common type for pastors attending our retreats is ENFP (extroverted, intuitive, feeling, perceiving). The second most common type for a pastor attending SonScape is the exact opposite type—ISTJ (introverted, sensing, thinking, judging). My point is that God calls all types of people into ministry! There is no one size that fits all.

Some pastors are great preachers. They can make God's Word come alive on a Sunday morning. But that same person may struggle with knowing how to administrate an organization. For others, administration comes naturally but preaching may be more difficult.

There are pastors who are compassionate caregivers. They remember people's names and stories. In a crisis they know exactly what to say and do. Other pastors hate making hospital visits and are always a little awkward when it comes to a crisis. But when it comes to vision casting or creating a strategic plan, they are in their "sweet spot."

I am a visionary and a dreamer. I can inspire people to believe the seemingly impossible is possible. But when it comes to follow-through and administration, I need some help. I am grateful for the people who have come alongside me in those areas, because they've helped make my ministry effective and exciting.

Pastors have different personalities, giftings, backgrounds, strengths, and weaknesses. There is no one pastor who can be what everyone in a congregation wants in a pastor. Far too often pastors burn themselves out trying to satisfy everyone's desires. It cannot be done. It should not even be attempted. In the end, what is lost is the pastor's own God-given, God-loved personality.

Affirm your pastor's interests and hobbies outside ministry. Let him know that as one church member you want your pastor to engage in those activities. His uniqueness goes beyond his pastoral gifts into the totality of life.

Some Ways You Can Help

1. **Gaining understanding and giving appreciation.** A new pastor will not be the same as the former pastor. He may be more gifted or less gifted but will not be the same. Comparisons help no one! Work to understand your pastor. Then offer appreciation in areas of strength and passion rather than criticisms about the things they lack. Appreciate them as unique individuals, not just pastors. If they like to fish, ask them about fishing. If their

love is music, talk to them about music. Let them know they are
more than a pastor in your eyes.

2. **Providing opportunities to develop both their strengths and
   areas where growth is needed.** There are so many great places
   to develop skills and techniques for ministry. Make sure your
   pastor has access to some of these educational opportunities. If
   the church budget does not allow this, perhaps a group of members could make it possible. PastorServe has some outstanding
   coaching and mentoring available. Criticism comes easy but is
   very limited in its benefit. Offering help for the betterment of a
   pastor can impact his life and ministry.

3. **Providing paid or volunteer staff in areas of weakness.** Who
   does your pastor need? Who has gifts that complement your
   pastor's? No one can do it all. Look for ways you can enable
   your pastor by supplying the help he needs. Do what you can
   personally and corporately.

Most Pastors Are Terrible at Self-Care

A good friend of mine was at a pastors' conference for our denomination. The pastor next to him was staring up at the mirrored ceiling in
the ballroom. Obviously the speaker was less than enthralling. Mark
looked up as well. The ceiling showed a room full of bald heads and
large stomachs. "This is God's view of our denomination's pastors,"
the pastor lamented.

Overall, pastors are not the physically healthiest group of people.
There is too much sitting and eating and not nearly enough exercising. Stress can become a way of life for many in ministry. Even in the

spiritual realm, pastors give more than they take in. Over time, their cup becomes empty and they have little left to give.

Author and pastor Jim Anderson wrote an article he called "Tale of Two Oswalds." Oswald Chambers, author of the beloved *My Utmost for His Highest*, was a chaplain in Cairo, Egypt, during World War I. Anderson quotes David McCasland's biography, which suggests a failure to rest may have contributed to Chambers's premature death from complications after an appendectomy.

> Photographs taken during the time show his face weathered and lined with fatigue. His sunken cheeks appear in marked contrast to his appearance two years before. Friends often expressed concern when he refused to rest during the midday heat.
>
> Many were asking, "Why?" Why had he waited so long for treatment? Why had he worked so long without rest, depleting his physical reserves to almost nothing?

Anderson suggests it may have been God's will to take Oswald Chambers home at age forty-three. But the questions asked by his loved ones are legitimate.

Anderson points also to Oswald Sanders, author of *Spiritual Leadership* and general director of China Inland Mission. Sanders came to value rest only after his zeal drove him to the edge of death itself.

> My life has been stress filled. I have done stupid things and have suffered for them. Way back about

> 50 years ago, I was under considerable stress … I
> began to lose weight and dropped 56 pounds. My
> wife would weep when I undressed at night seeing
> this old bag of bones.[1]

It was a doctor who told Sanders, "There is only one thing that will recuperate nervous exhaustion, and that is rest and sleep. It is the way you build up your reserves again and are able to serve the Lord effectively."

Sanders listened and lived to the age of eighty-nine. He often shared what he had learned with young Christian leaders: "I am not suggesting for a moment that you become overly solicitous for yourself or care for yourself too much or be afraid to spend. *But there is a point when it is wise to stop and have a rest.*"[2]

The story of the two Oswalds has been repeated across the decades. Well-known Christian leaders like Peter Scazzero (*The Emotionally Healthy Church*), Fil Anderson (*Running on Empty*), and Wayne Cordeiro (*Leading on Empty*) have had to learn the hard way. There are also thousands of names we will never know because they wore themselves out and left the ministry.

Self-care is a primary focus of SonScape Retreats. It is something that is both talked about and experienced during our week together. It is amazing how many pastors have little to no concept of the importance of managing the many aspects of their lives. As a result, the physical, emotional, and spiritual health of pastors today is poor at best. Self-care is not selfish; it is for one's own sake as well as the sake of the people served. It does not mean pastors do not work hard. It is rather about a rhythm of working hard and then resting well so that they can accomplish the tasks God has given them to do.

Some Ways You Can Help

1. **Encouraging time away to live life and have fun.** Sometimes simple encouragement can be what God uses to help a pastor from time to time. I have met pastors who love to play the piano, but they never do. Some pastors love to work with wood, but they have not touched their tools in months. God loves to watch pastors use their nonpastoral gifts—whether music, sports, woodworking, or gardening. "Are you playing the piano?" "Have you been to a ball game recently?" "How is your garden coming along?" A little encouragement can go further than you know.

2. **Making places to get away available.** As I write these words, I am sitting on the balcony overlooking the Atlantic Ocean in Florida. It is a spectacular day! I will write for a while and then head down to the beach. Barbara and I are here because my aunt, uncle, and cousin have made it available to us. What a gift. In every church body there is someone who has a place somewhere. In every church there is someone, or a group of people, who has the ability to buy airline tickets if needed. Developing new and much-needed patterns of self-care is difficult in the midst of life and ministry. It takes going away, getting some rest, having time to reflect on oneself.

3. **Purchasing a membership at a health club and encouraging its use.** When a pastor is exercising regularly, it is a benefit personally and to the church as a whole. You may even want

to invest in a personal trainer. For most pastors, exercise falls low on the priority scale, so your encouragement can make the difference.

4. **Making sure your pastor has an annual physical.** Physical health is a part of true spiritual health. Making an annual physical an expectation of the job can be good for everyone.

Healthy pastors are those who know how to separate between who they are and what they do. They take time for grieving, counseling, self-discovery, and *rest*. They play often and laugh much.

A Cowboy Pastor—Part 2

Scott and Diane spent their week rethinking many parts of their lives and ministry. For the first time in a long while they rested and played. In our private times together they shared, and we gently guided. In it all, God brought clarity.

Scott still struggles with his drivenness, but he now has tools to keep it in balance. They take time for rest and play. Diane has climbed all fifty-two fourteen-thousand-foot mountains in Colorado and published a journal of her adventures. Scott owns horses again. He rides for pleasure and even competes nationally in riding and roping events.

They came back to SonScape for a refresher retreat a few years after their first experience and have since learned the importance of coming away from time to time.

They have planted a new church in Wyoming. Life and ministry are still full and intense. But at the end of the day, Scott comes home and sits in his easy chair. Scott and Diane do not have it all together, but they are healthier and are enjoying both life and ministry more.

It was a group of church leaders who stepped in, even against Scott's desires, and made the difference. They may have saved Scott's ministry. While they wanted Scott to be a healthy pastor, even more they wanted him to be a healthy person. When a congregation invests in their pastor as a person, the result is often a healthier pastor and a healthier church.

Chapter 3

Pastor Superman
Managing Expectations

In 2004, Barbara and our two younger kids, Lucas and Hillary, rafted the upper Nile River in Uganda, Africa. When most people think of the Nile, they think of the wide, slow-moving river as it approaches the delta at the Mediterranean Sea.

The upper Nile is much different. Its white water is extraordinary, beyond anything in North America. The many class-five rapids are violent, sometimes dropping fifteen to twenty feet in a very short distance. Barbara, Lucas, and Hillary were often thrown from their raft along with their guide.

Kayaks, traveling on either side of the raft, would work to rescue waterlogged rafters, returning them to safety. Barbara says it was the wildest ride of her life. Lucas says it was the biggest rush he has experienced.

Living amid the expectations of denomination and congregation is like riding the white water of the upper Nile River for many pastors—driven along, out of control, head just barely above water. Rather than an exciting adventure, it becomes a survival course. Of the many types of currents that can threaten ministries, the current of expectations is often the most dangerous.

"How did I get here?" It is a common question asked by pastors at our retreats. It may refer to fatigue, burnout, depression, doubt, or even moral failure. Whatever the "here" refers to, expectations are often the current that carried them to that destination. Learning to navigate the current of expectations is essential for the health of a pastor. Rarely are expectations not mentioned among the most difficult parts of a pastor's work with people and the church.

A Helpful Exercise

What are your top twenty expectations for your pastor? Write them down quickly without analyzing each one. Take a few minutes to reflect on your list. Read each one aloud, listening to how each sounds as you hear it. How many of your expectations are realistic? Is it reasonable to think that one person can accomplish your list of expectations? Could *you* meet them all?

Now multiply your list by the number of people that attend your church. Some of the expectations will be the same as yours, but not all of them. The list grows longer with each person. Are you getting a sense of why what's expected of your pastor can be out of control?

Where do your and others' expectations come from? Do you think any individual man or woman should be able to accomplish such a list? A list that might include:

- Our former pastor was always available.
- When I was growing up, our pastor was so caring and friendly.

- I once heard a pastor who preached with amazing passion and inspiration.
- Our previous pastor's children were so obedient, and his wife was involved in everything.

Expectations can also come from idealistic and completely unrealistic pictures of a pastor that lie in the mind of each member of the congregation.

- I think a really great pastor would preach a "home-run sermon" every Sunday.
- I think a truly compassionate pastor should know all my children, even if our church has grown to over a thousand people.
- Great pastors are gifted in evangelism and outreach, without changing the culture and "feeling" of the church.
- I once read a book about a pastor who gave 50 percent of his salary back to his church and God really blessed his ministry.

Whatever the expectations and wherever they come from, the issue is whether they are reasonable and helpful. Regardless if they are spoken or unspoken, unreasonable expectations leave a pastor feeling grossly inadequate and become a barrier to effective ministry. They usurp the legitimate role of the pastor.

Someone shared with me this humorous but telling job description of the perfect pastor:

- The perfect pastor preaches exactly ten minutes every Sunday.
- He condemns sin but never hurts anyone's feelings.
- He works from 8:00 a.m. to 10:00 p.m. every day but has plenty of time off to be with his family.
- He is thirty-nine years old but has forty years of experience.
- He knows all his people by name but spends most of his time studying and praying.
- He knows when people are sick or in need of visitation even without anyone telling him.
- The perfect pastor is content making five hundred dollars a week and wears beautiful but appropriate clothing to all events.
- The perfect pastor has a burning desire to work with teenagers but spends all his time with seniors.

You get the idea!

Expectations Can Kill Your Pastor

Brian was a young pastor called to serve churches in Africa. Brian and his wife, Jill, were young and passionate. A church in the States was their primary source of support and care, and a missions committee was responsible for monthly care and contact.

Brian and Jill had just begun their first furlough after four years in Africa when they were called in to meet with the committee. The committee had come to the collected opinion that Brian and Jill were not working hard enough and that they were abusing their time, so they had decided to drop their support—completely. They had based their decision on several events, with two in particular. First, Brian had decided to stay with Jill in the capital city while she was hospitalized with a difficult pregnancy and where better care could be offered. The committee thought Brian should have stayed at the mission four hours away. Second, Brian had at one time requested a few days off to take a spiritual retreat. In the end the committee simply did not want them as missionaries any longer because of the perception that Brian and Jill were just not working as hard as they should have been.

When this couple walked into our retreat center, they felt as though they had been blindsided by a semitruck and weren't sure they could recover. I have come to know this couple well across the years, and I can assure you they are anything but lazy!

By the way, not one member of that missions committee had ever served on the mission field. I have often wondered: Could their expectations ever have been attained? How many other young couples were crushed under their demands?

Eventually, Brian and Jill returned to Africa supported by a different church that knew how to love and encourage missionary pastors. They served over fifteen years in Africa, planting many churches, helping to start a seminary for indigenous pastors, and winning many for Jesus.

Like Brian and Jill, many young pastors have been overwhelmed by the current of people's complex and unreasonable expectations. This is not to say that pastors are always right and people are always wrong. I certainly learned from the people I served. More than once they taught me things I needed to know about life and faith. Caring people always contribute to the development of a young pastor.

Have you ever worked for one hundred bosses? Sounds ridiculous, right? Yet many pastors feel like that is their world. Some want their pastor to focus more on evangelism. Some want better administration and organization. There are those who expect more time spent on the Sunday service. Parents want a great children and youth program. The elderly want more personal visitation. The expectations go on and on.

In the first chapter of the gospel of Mark, we have a glimpse into the ministry life of Jesus. In Capernaum, Jesus drove out a demon and the people were amazed. News of His actions and authority spread throughout the region. In verses 32–33 we read:

> That evening at sundown they brought to [Jesus]
> all who were sick or oppressed by demons. And the
> whole city was gathered together at the door.

Pastors understand those words. Too often they feel as if the whole church is seeking something from them.

- Fix my husband.
- Agree with my position.
- Answer my question.
- Give me hope.
- Tell me what to do.
- Bring my child back to faith.

Most expectations put on the pastor by church members are thought to be, at least by the ones bringing the expectations, within the norm of what you should expect. But there is often a group that seeks to have the lion's share of influence and control in the church. Some are long-term members going back decades or even generations. Others hold the purse strings. Their contributions are significant but with conditions attached. More than love and support, their expectations appear as a need to control.

Pastors can feel as though they are connecting with 95 percent of the congregation but failing with the 5 percent who are the power brokers in the church. Many pastors feel ill equipped to manage these difficult and conflictive relationships. It has been our experience at SonScape Retreats that too many pastors are fired or forced out of a church by a very small, very influential group of people. When a strong group of people comes against a pastor with their long list of unreasonable expectations, it can be overwhelming and defeating.

When power brokers control a church and the majority remain silent, pastors will either become puppets or they will last a few years at best. Gifted, committed young pastors leave ministry every month, "crucified" by the few and not defended by the many. Sounds like a familiar Bible story of a crucifixion where a few pulled it off and many simply went along.

There is a well-known website (expastors.com) specifically for ex-pastors to decompress and discuss their experiences, and there are a lot of former pastors who participate in the conversation. I don't always agree with everything I've read there, but I agree with quite a bit of it. One of the interesting discussions had to do with whether the role of pastor as we know it today is possible or even biblical. I do know that far too often we are setting men and women up for failure by putting them in a role that borders on the impossible. In this seemingly impossible position we also fail to give them adequate tools and support. I have personally met many of the "victims" of this flawed system. They are remarkable men and women who are barely keeping their heads above water in the raging current of expectations.

Expectations within the Pastor

Expectations on pastors can come from many sources: denominational leaders, community members, their congregation, and even other pastors they know. But many times the combined sum of all those external expectations do not compare to the internal expectations pastors place on themselves. Let me say that again in case you missed it! *The combined total of all the external expectations often do not compare to the internal expectations a pastor places upon himself or herself.*

There are too many pastors trying to find their worth and value in their performance. Their focus is on doing and succeeding. They cannot stop. Burdens that are not theirs to carry take them to the point of collapse, but they just keep going.

Such was a pastor who attended a SonScape Retreat a few years ago. He could not rest and he could not stop. There was neither the time nor the ability to come away and be still. God intervened dramatically during his days at our retreat. Near the end of the week he shared a memory with us—a vivid memory.

In fourth grade he was struggling. He had been sick a lot that year, and he was falling behind in school. He was asked to stand out in the hallway as his parents and teacher met together. After a time he was called into the classroom, and his father pulled up one of the small chairs, sat down, and looked him squarely in the eye. Calling him by name, his father said, "If you fail fourth grade, you will never succeed in anything and you will be a failure all your life."

Something happened in that conversation. From that day on, he put his life in hyperdrive. He passed fourth grade. He was valedictorian in high school and in college. Life became about excelling and succeeding in everything. He had no idea when to throttle back or put the brakes on. Enough was never enough. His church was going well, but he had lost all joy in life and ministry.

At SonScape Retreats we believe that in the front of every pastor's Bible, perhaps even across their bathroom mirror, these words should be written in bold letters: *There is a Savior, and you are not Him.*

Pastors cannot solve every person's problems nor meet every person's need. If they try, they will be carried away by the raging current of their own expectations.

You cannot control the expectations that whirl within your pastor. But you can recognize that pastors struggle like all people, with faulty thinking and messed-up emotions. Pastors are human.

You cannot control the internal expectations that might plague your pastor, but you can help. You can make sure your pastor has access to good counseling and good coaching. You can encourage your pastor to take time for emotional health and make adequate tools and resources available. Above all, you can pray!

Time Away Is Essential

After a particularly intense time of ministry recorded in Mark 6:30–31, the disciples were overwhelmed by expectations, both internal and external.

> The apostles returned to Jesus and told him all that
> they had done and taught. And he said to them,
> "Come away by yourselves to a desolate place and
> rest a while."

Pastors understand how ministry can become so overwhelming that there is not even time to eat. Crises, sermon preparation, hospital visits, counseling sessions, staff meetings, board meetings, denominational activities, financial needs, and much more consume the day, the month, and the year. Because of the pace and the pressure of ministry, time away is essential.

But as we continue, we see Jesus had the answer:

> And he said to them, "Come away by yourselves to
> a desolate place and rest a while."

Many times in the Gospels, Jesus went away to a quiet place to rest and to pray. His ministry was intense, people's needs were consuming, the cross lay just ahead—so Jesus often retreated to be with His heavenly Father and to rest. And He taught His disciples to do the same.

Rest is talked about much in the Scriptures. Clearly God knew that if we keep running and running and running, we will lose our way. Pastors need to come away with Jesus to a quiet place to get some rest so they can return refreshed and renewed for the opportunities ministry presents. Days off and vacation can be part of this process, but so can spiritual retreats.

Spiritual retreats offer your pastor a time to recalibrate their thinking and their ministry. Time to make sure that the expectations of people and self are not driving their lives but rather God's desires and purposes. These times away were essential for Jesus and they are essential for your pastor.

Conferences and seminars are good for developing tools and skills, but they are not spiritual retreats. In a spiritual retreat your pastor makes time for prayer, reflection, and sometimes guided conversation. These times are critical for your pastor, but they are often pushed aside by the currents of expectations and needs.

"But I don't get times to come away! Life gets overwhelming for me too. You're saying I need to make sure my pastor has what I don't?" Exactly—especially if we expect our pastors to be there for us when we are in a place we can't go on alone; a place where we need his presence, his encouragement, his wisdom, and his spiritual guidance.

Remember Barbara rafting the Nile? On either side of the raft was a kayak. The kayaks were there to rescue waterlogged rafters when they were thrown into the rapids. In the turbulent rapids of life, one of the kayaks alongside you is manned by your pastor. Sometimes he is calling out to you with words of biblical insight, but other times he reaches out a hand and pulls you to safety. He is there for you, but he needs you to invest in him. Only together can you each be what the other needs.

Are There Reasonable Expectations?

Not only are there reasonable expectations—I would use the word *essential* expectations. Every pastor needs a list of essential expectations. Too often the problem is that neither the church membership nor the pastor has thought through what those essentials might be, nor have they communicated them to each other.

As you think about essential expectations, there are two cautions to keep in mind. First, a list of reasonable expectations that becomes too long will become unreasonable. A single person must be able to accomplish the list in a regular workweek. Google the definition of the word *unreasonable* and here is what you will find:

> Not reasonable or rational; acting at variance with or
> contrary to reason; not guided by reason or sound
> judgment; irrational.[1]

I am convinced that a clear and reasonable list of expectations for the pastor, by your church, would eliminate many unnecessary criticisms and conflicts. That is why I prefer using the words *essential expectations*. What does your congregation want from your pastor first and foremost? Without such a list, written out and agreed upon, both pastor and church will be frustrated.

The second caution is that the list of expectations must take into account the personality and gifting of your pastor. It is unreasonable to expect something that is far outside what your pastor can do. That is why it is necessary for there to be an understanding of the uniqueness of your pastor. To expect of people what they cannot do sets them up for failure.

Barbara and I were asked to work with a ministry team in conflict. The team was made up of some remarkably gifted and committed people. But the team members were very frustrated with the team leader and the team leader with them.

Jay was a strategic leader with a clear direction for the ministry. The team he led had all agreed on the vision and the goals. There was much to be done. The team had come to see Jay as unsympathetic and uncaring, focused only on the work of the ministry. Jay had come to see the team as whiners, always wanting his time and attention for secondary issues.

As we talked together, the team realized it was not that Jay did not care but that he was wired to accomplish goals and to make things happen. Many members of the team wanted him to be the team caregiver. That was just not going to happen, at least not to the level they desired.

In the end it was decided that Jay would take the responsibility as the strategic leader and that other team members would assume the caregiving roles. Several months later we received an email from Jay saying the team was really clicking and that he loved his job.

Does your church know what the essential expectations are for your pastor? Are they written and reviewed regularly?

The Gift of Those Willing to Share the Load

"What can I do to help, Pastor?"

Seven words that are music to every pastor's ears. They are words that convey not expectation but partnership. "I am in this with you, Pastor—you can count on me!"

The church I served in Maple Grove, Minnesota, was full of people willing to share the load. I was blessed by partners in ministry. There I learned to have people come alongside you when the currents of expectations rage around you. I also learned that there are some who, rather than asking the question of how to help, simply see the need and respond to it.

There are also those who are always around to help. Like Aaron and Hur they see and respond. They are the salt of the earth. They are the gift that makes ministry possible. Every church has them, some more than others. On behalf of pastors serving all over the world, if you are one of these individuals—thank you! You are a blessing!

But there is one more category of people within the church: those who really care, who want to help, but never step forward. They never ask the question, and they never respond to the need. They may feel they don't have the time, or they are not capable enough, or they just let someone else do it.

What a difference if pastors and the people they serve would join together with realistic expectations and a commitment to help one another. Our churches would become more of what God intended and what we all deeply desire.

A Second Exercise

We started this chapter with an exercise. Let me suggest another. Write down five things your pastor can expect from you.

Does your pastor know them? Have you ever told him? Maybe you need to write a note or even sit down with your pastor face to face. It will mean more to your pastor than you can imagine. Let your pastor know you are standing with him.

Maybe you even need to ask for forgiveness for the expectations you have placed on him that you now realize were either unrealistic or unfair. Sure, it may be hard, but it will make a huge difference for you and an even greater difference for your pastor.

Every pastor knows ministry is not easy. But when people come alongside, when they recognize and admit wrong expectations, and when they ask forgiveness—a pastor's heart comes alive.

Five things. Name them. Share them with your pastor. Commit to them. Grab a paddle, and jump into the raft!

So let's recap where you can lend a hand to your pastor as he faces a seemingly unending onslaught of expectations:

1. **Understand what your pastor faces in regard to expectations.** You have taken a huge step in reading this book. As we have said, your pastor is a rare individual with gifts and struggles unique to him. So many in ministry desire to have someone understand the pressures and problems they face. You cannot solve your pastor's struggles, but an occasional spoken or written word can be an incredible encouragement to a pastor in the midst of battle.

2. **Look hard and deep at your own expectations for your pastor.** You are only one person in the congregation, but you are one person! Taking the time to examine your own thoughts and expectations, and adjusting those that are unrealistic or just plain wrong, is significant. Your willingness to tell your pastor what you have discovered about the expectations he faces, and

even asking forgiveness, if appropriate, can go a long way in encouraging the one who leads your church.

3. **Encourage your church leaders to develop and publicize the essential expectations of your pastor.** Let the church know what is expected from your pastor. Other things are secondary. They will need to be accomplished by volunteers or wait until other staff can be hired.

4. **Speak up against unrealistic expectations.** From time to time you may have the opportunity to address unrealistic expectations by people in the church, or even the church as a whole. Most do not understand how much it means when someone says to a group of people *what the pastors themselves cannot say*.

5. **Ask your pastor how you can help, and look for ways beyond his answers.** Pastors are not used to people asking how they can help. They may or may not have a good answer, but ask anyway. Then look for things you can do as well.

6. **Tell your pastor what he can expect of you, and then follow through.** Words are valuable but only when they are followed by action. Show your pastor you are with him by the things you do.

7. **Encourage times away for your pastor.** Encouraging your pastor to step away to process life and ministry can be extremely helpful both to pastor and to church. Pastors often feel guilty for time focused on self. When church leaders and church members encourage such times of personal growth and reflection, it can have a profound impact.

Chapter 4

Capacity
It's Limited

Paul's heart was conflicted. In many ways, he felt as if he were about to take the first step in a journey he knew would end in tragedy. And yet the pull on his emotions to proceed was overwhelming.

Paul and his wife, Sheila, were close to accepting the call to lead an established Texas church. After a dozen years on the West Coast, they were excited to return home to Dallas, where they had both been born, been raised, attended school, and fell in love. With four children in tow, this was the perfect opportunity to move close to both sets of grandparents, close friends, a familiar environment, and their beloved Cowboys.

Everything seemed perfect. Paul had pastored a California church well, first in the role of discipleship pastor and for the past seven years in the role of lead pastor. The longer they spent in California, the greater the desire to return to Texas grew until they sensed they could no longer ignore it. When the lead pastor abruptly retired at Paul's parents' church, everything seemed to fit. A church of twenty-five hundred, they made Paul their first choice after an eight-month search that had resulted in more than two hundred applications. As the search process narrowed, Paul and Sheila made two trips to the church, the second with the entire family. Sheila was thrilled to have the children close to grandparents, the children couldn't wait to be near grandparents, and Paul was excited to lead a growing, dynamic church with a solid staff, a commitment to community transformation, and a young congregation.

Paul looked over the final offer from the church, and he again reviewed the lead pastor job description. As he read through each responsibility, he jotted down anticipated hours next to each item. Preach in Sunday morning worship service a minimum of forty-five times a year. Paul knew that his lengthy sermon preparation was a weekly minimum of twenty hours. Lead weekly staff meeting and worship planning meeting and supervise five direct reports added another ten hours. Lead the weekly elder prayer gathering, the bimonthly elder meeting, and the monthly deacons meeting added another five hours. Paul knew that the expectation of hospital visits, weekly counseling, leadership training, and open office hours would easily add another twelve hours to his week. Paul and Sheila were to be members of a weekly missional community (small group) that, to his relief, Paul wouldn't lead. The church hosted a monthly gathering of local pastors during which time Paul would serve as host. He would be expected to enthusiastically participate in denominational gatherings, locally, regionally, and nationally. And then there were the unwritten expectations. The former pastor had written several books that helped to place the church on the national landscape, and Paul would be expected to do the same.

Paul reviewed the job description over and over again. As he added the numbers he had placed next to each lead pastor responsibility, the total came to eighty-two. Surely he had overestimated the time it would take to fulfill each responsibility. Perhaps he could complete his sermon preparation in twelve hours. Perhaps the staff meetings could be cut from ninety minutes to sixty. Perhaps this wouldn't be a needy congregation. Paul knew better, but against every instinct in his spirit, he called the chairman of the search committee and said yes, he would come.

Pastoral Capacity

An exaggerated story? Hardly. This story is repeated daily in churches across the United States and around the world. The expectations placed on the pastor are wildly unrealistic (as Larry detailed in the previous chapter). As a result, pastors are experiencing burnout at alarming rates. What is the heart of the problem?

Simply stated, everyone has limited capacity. Read that again. Stated another way, *no one* (which includes your pastor) *possesses unlimited capacity.* Everyone has 168 hours per week in which to work, sleep, eat, love their spouse, love their children, invest in personal relationships, minister to the lost, exercise, relax, and perform many other activities. Picture a bank that credits your account with 86,400 dollars every morning. Great news, right? And yet, there is one catch. Every night at midnight the bank deletes whatever part of the balance you failed to spend during the day. What would you do? Draw out every cent, of course! Each of us has such a bank. Its name is *time.* It allows no overdraft. Each day, it opens a new account for you. If you fail to use that day's deposits, the loss is yours.

In the case of a pastor, if his time is well managed, he can lead the church, love his spouse and children, exercise five mornings a week, get a healthy amount of sleep, engage in redemptive relationships, eat, rest, and effectively participate in the remainder of activities that make up an average week. And yet the unknown and the unexpected inevitably creep into every week. For example, when a child is injured and requires a late-night trip to the emergency room, you predictably get less sleep. Or, if you catch up on sleep, it may result in you having fewer hours to work. Every activity drains already limited capacity. When a marriage is in crisis, you spend additional time with your spouse that may lead to less time exercising or working. In everything we do, there is a trade-off. We just can't magically add hours to our week. We all live our lives within limited capacity.

The problem for the pastor is accentuated when we begin with a job description rather than a person's capacity to *fulfill a job description*. It's worth noting that this is not true just for pastors but for anyone who operates under the boundaries of a job description.

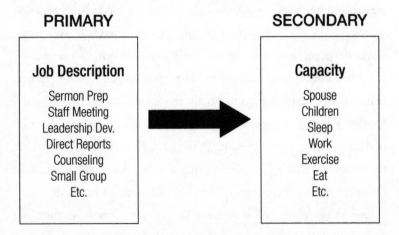

When we begin with a job description as the foundation (see diagram), believing this to be a pastor's primary ministry, we are unknowingly asking and expecting the pastor to cheat some aspect of his secondary responsibilities (which is, in reality, *his primary responsibility*). If you expect your pastor to work more than sixty hours per week (as more than one-third of pastors do), you will limit some area of his life that will die apart from the investment of time. In the case of Paul, he determined that to fulfill the job description, even with reduced sermon preparation time, it would take a minimum of seventy hours per week. Add that to the fifty-two hours needed for sleep, five hours to exercise, time to shower and eat, and there would be precious little time remaining for his spouse, his children, any form of recreation, and Sabbath. Paul knew the pastoral position would end in tragedy because someone would be greatly disappointed. Either the church would be frustrated with Paul's leadership deficit (because he would fulfill only a portion of his job description) or his family would be frustrated with the dearth of time given to his loved ones. From day one, Paul was set up to fail. He might fail in his role as a pastor, or he might fail in his role as a husband and a father, but one way or another, Paul would fail. *Because of unrealistic job descriptions, the majority of pastors are set up to fail, which is one of the primary contributors to the pastoral crisis we are presently experiencing in America and around the world.*

Family Is a Pastor's Primary Ministry

As I have mentioned elsewhere, the most common call we receive at PastorServe revolves around the challenge of balancing family and ministry. The dilemma commonly sounds something like this: "I'm struggling to balance family and ministry. There is an unresolvable tension between the seemingly unending demands of my ministry and the time I know I should be spending with my family. I don't know how to resolve the tension, and I feel like it is ripping my family apart! I feel as if I have no boundaries in my role as a pastor. While I understand my family can't live in isolation, I am struggling with my commitment to say yes to the ministry and my commitment to say yes to my family. I am finding it difficult, if not impossible, to spend an appropriate, healthy amount of time with my family without feeling incredibly guilty, like I am cheating the church."

Our response has been the same for nearly two decades (and pastors, this may change your life). We gently remind the pastor: *While we appreciate the tension and the reason behind the question, you are thinking of the issue in an unbiblical paradigm. All of life is ministry, and your family is your primary ministry.* Read that last sentence again.

Practically, what does this mean? It means that when a pastor leaves the church office to spend time at his daughter's soccer game, he is not walking away from the ministry to spend time with his family. He is leaving his secondary ministry to spend time in his primary ministry. As a church leader, if you believe this, it will fundamentally change the way you deal with your pastor.

Tragically, I have watched leaders of churches allow their pastor to operate in a destructive cycle of work, primarily because to create pastoral boundaries highlights their own deficiencies—which leads to an overwhelming sense of guilt and shame.

All too often, when I meet with a church leader, the conversation goes something like this: "I would encourage you to create boundaries which will allow your pastor to regularly spend time with his wife and his children. The fact that he regularly works a seventy-hour week is going to ultimately bring irreparable harm to his marriage." The leader responds, "While I understand what you are saying, personally, I work more than eighty hours each week. I am away from home an average of three nights each week, and I'm not sure how I can recommend something for my pastor that I, and the majority of church leaders, don't experience ourselves." What the elder is saying is because he is personally failing in this area, he would feel better if *everyone* failed in the area. Or, stated another way, mass failure is easier to bear than singular failure. *God help the church!*

When working through the job description of any pastor, *always begin with capacity* (see the following diagram). How much time do you want your pastor to spend nurturing his marriage and his family, his primary ministry? How much time should be spent sleeping, exercising, and relaxing? While this prioritization may sound upside down in light of the workplace you may experience, keep in mind that the issue with your pastor is not laziness! The problem is the tendency to overextend to the point of severe damage.

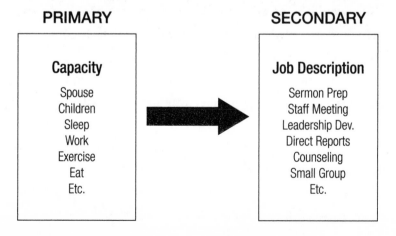

PRIMARY

Capacity

Spouse
Children
Sleep
Work
Exercise
Eat
Etc.

SECONDARY

Job Description

Sermon Prep
Staff Meeting
Leadership Dev.
Direct Reports
Counseling
Small Group
Etc.

When a local church holds to a biblical understanding of capacity, it will free their pastor to live out his calling with his whole heart before an audience of One. It is a win-win! *We could slow the avalanche of pastoral burnout if we freed our pastors from the shackles of unrealistic job descriptions that inevitably lead to disillusionment, failure, and the departure from pastoral ministry.*

At PastorServe, after working with thousands of pastors from all fifty states and several countries around the world, we have concluded that a healthy pastoral workweek is in the range of forty-eight to fifty-two hours per week. In fact, experience has taught us that once a pastor (or anyone) hits fifty-two hours of work per week, the quality of work begins to decline significantly.

This is not a recent discovery. Henry Ford understood this. In 1914, he changed his workforce from a nine-hour workday to an eight-hour workday. Then in 1926, he adjusted from a six-day workweek to a five-day workweek. Ford believed the result would be greater production in shorter hours. He was right, and the forty-hour workweek was born. The lessons from Henry Ford should not be lost on our pastors.

As I (Jimmy) was writing this chapter, Larry reminded me of the fact that we are not suggesting pastors should not work hard. We believe pastors are called to give their very best. We are suggesting that there must be a balance between working hard and resting well so that, once again, we can work hard.

Without a healthy balance between work and rest, the life of the pastor will eventually spiral into disaster.

Extending Grace to Your Pastor

Practically, as a member of a local church, don't be so hard on your pastor if he isn't able to immediately schedule an appointment with you. Remember, his capacity is limited. Your pastor may have ten hours built into his week to connect with members of the congregation. In many large churches, that may mean a three-month wait to personally meet with the pastor. *Don't be frustrated! Don't threaten to leave the church unless the pastor fits you into his schedule.* Understand that if the pastor were to give in to your demand for an immediate meeting to discuss your frustrations, you have just reduced his nonwork capacity for that day. Because of the additional time spent addressing your concerns, he *will* sacrifice something. It may be an hour at the gym, the first half of his son's basketball game, a walk with his wife, or a good night's sleep, but *something will be sacrificed!* And when this is repeated day after day, destructive patterns begin to work their way into the pastor's life.

I have dealt with disgruntled church members who have expressed tremendous frustration with their pastors' perceived unwillingness to address a pressing issue. This is particularly common in larger churches. When I ask if they have attempted to contact one of the other dozen pastors in the church, they assure me that only the lead pastor is equipped to address this particular predicament. The other pastors do not possess the spiritual maturity or expertise to effectively tackle the crisis. In this case, I can assure you the problem does not lie with the pastor.

I often visit churches where, after the message, the congregation is informed that the speaker, several pastors, and elders will be available at the front to pray with and for people. Dozens of people line up asking the preacher to pray for them, while other pastors (many who are much more gifted) stand idly by. When someone from the leadership moves through the line informing people that there are a number of pastors willing to pray for them, they defensively let the person know that they *must* speak with the morning speaker, as if only he will understand the problem. It's as if they are saying that only his prayers carry the power of the Holy Spirit. It is this mind-set that drains pastoral capacity. Only the lead pastor can counsel me. Only the lead pastor can marry my daughter. Only the lead pastor can perform the funeral service for my mother.

If you are a church member who is convinced that only the lead pastor possesses the gifts to address your needs, you have a severe case of pastoral superstar syndrome. Get over it! You may be unknowingly destroying your pastor by reducing his capacity!

Two-Dimensional Capacity

Patrick and Graham have worked together for six years. With similar job descriptions, they are expected to produce similar results while working roughly the same amount of hours. They both enjoy their roles within the team and are viewed positively by their workplace peers. Yet at the conclusion of each week, when Patrick and Graham discuss outcomes of their work, there is regularly a considerable discrepancy in their workplace production. Despite the fact that they each work a fifty-hour week, Graham regularly accomplishes 25 percent more than Patrick. Additionally, Graham seems to find the time to enjoy activities with his wife, attend concerts and sporting events, and still have margin for relationships with a number of close friends. Patrick struggles to mow the yard. If both share identical boundaries of time, how is Graham able to accomplish so much more?

Properly understood, capacity is not one dimensional but two dimensional. There is a significant difference between the breadth (168 hours per week) and the depth (how we use the 168 hours per week) of one's capacity. After all, if we each have 168 hours in one week, then how do some people seem to possess the amazing ability to accomplish a great deal while others struggle to achieve the basics? How is Graham able to accomplish so much more than Patrick?

While it is true that no one possesses the ability to change the breadth of capacity, to varying degrees we *can* impact the depth of our capacity. There are a number of factors that impact the depth of our capacity, one of which is worthy of further discussion.

Capacity Extenders

Externally, we can extend the depth of our capacity by asking others to perform tasks that we determine would save us time if another performed them. In other words, *financial capacity impacts clock capacity*. In the United States, we do it nearly every day. For example, we ask someone to change the oil in our car because it saves us the time we would have spent doing it ourselves. We may hire a CPA to file our taxes because it isn't worth it to take the time to file taxes on our own. If you are blessed to live in a home with a yard, you may have someone who takes care of your lawn. You may even have a maid and a nanny. You may fly to your vacation destination rather than drive. You may have a contractor who takes care of every minor home repair. Unquestionably, some are blessed with the financial means to extend the depths of their capacities.

The problem emerges when those who possess the means to maximize capacity compare their schedules to those who do not possess the means to increase the depth of their capacities. You and your pastor may each work a fifty-hour workweek. And yet you cannot understand why he is not able to spend an adequate amount of time with his wife and children when you are able to find large blocks of time to engage with your family. But when you look closer, your pastor mows his yard, does the majority of home repairs, and prepares his own taxes. You flew your family to the beach for a one-week vacation while your pastor's family took three days of their vacation to drive to and from the beach. If you are fortunate enough to possess the financial means to create margin, don't blindly expect that of others who do not share your financial blessing. On the other end of the financial spectrum, others may not have the resources to extend capacity, but they do possess the time. Pastors often lose on both ends.

Years ago PastorServe was given a financial gift from a donor who asked us to bless pastors during the summer months. We thought it was a brilliant idea to target a specific group of pastors—young church planters, to whom we offered a nice dinner and a movie. Who wouldn't take us up on such a generous offer? And yet, in reality, very few pastors accepted the gift. We made some calls to find out why. The answer was so simple we were embarrassed we hadn't seen it. Pastors weren't accepting the offer because they lacked the financial capacity to accept the offer! Nearly every young couple had young children, and a night out meant

(1) finding a babysitter and (2) finding the funds to pay a babysitter to watch their children. Some couples with three or four children informed us that babysitting for an evening away would run them close to fifty dollars. Ironically, they simply couldn't afford to receive our gift! After some further discussion, we modified our offer. We offered pastors a date night that included a nice dinner, a movie, *and childcare*. Let the floodgates open! Megan and Sarah, my two oldest daughters, spent many nights that summer in pastors' homes watching their children. Pastors were elated. We heard story after story about how it was wonderful to be blessed with a gift and, by providing childcare, creating the capacity to enjoy the gift.

I could tell stories about pastors who were discouraged when they received two tickets to an event from a member of their church. Think about it: "We just received two tickets to a great concert. While we are so excited to go, we know that the amount of time and money it will take to arrange for childcare almost makes it impossible. We will need to find someone to stay at home with our two-year-old while someone else picks up our five-year-old from soccer and our seven-year-old from piano. Honestly, it will take three people to get everyone where they need to go. While we may be able to find friends to help with the two older children, we will need to pay for a babysitter. And the amount of stress this places on my wife and me feels overwhelming. We simply don't possess the capacity to enjoy the gift! The couple who gave us the tickets are wonderful people! They have been a faithful part of our church for years. To avoid offending them, we feel obligated to attend the concert. But the financial and emotional cost will be high."

Capacity depth fluctuates in different seasons of life. Depth increases when you are single, when you don't have children, and when you experience the empty nest. It increases if your last name is Rockefeller, Buffett, or Gates. Be sensitive to your pastor's season of life. When he has no children at home, spending three nights out a week might not be too much to ask. If he has children at home, three nights a week away from home could bring his family to the breaking point. A generous offer for your pastor to join you at an event may strain his capacity. Remember, your situation is not your pastor's situation. Be sensitive to his unique challenges.

Capacity and the Holy Spirit

In an earlier book, *Survive or Thrive: Six Relationships Every Pastor Needs*, I told a story about the time I traveled to Grass Valley, California, to meet with Glenn, a leader well known for his wisdom. After hearing of my struggle to slow down and take the necessary time to pour into my marriage and family, Glenn took me to John chapter 5. He then guided me through a discussion of the importance of seeking and following the leading of the Holy Spirit. And although the Holy Spirit is not mentioned in this passage, He is actually all over it. John 5:3–9 presents Jesus coming to the pools at Bethesda, an infirmary to thousands of desperate, needy people looking for a miracle. John tells us:

> In these lay a multitude of invalids—blind, lame,
> and paralyzed. One man was there who had been
> an invalid for thirty-eight years. When Jesus saw

him lying there and knew that he had already been there a long time, he said to him, "Do you want to be healed?" The sick man answered him, "Sir, I have no one to put me into the pool when the water is stirred up, and while I am going another steps down before me." Jesus said to him, "Get up, take up your bed, and walk." And at once the man was healed, and he took up his bed and walked.

From what we understand from John's account, Jesus went to Bethesda, where there were a multitude of extreme needs. We can only speculate as to the size of the crowd that "multitude" describes, but it was likely several thousand. This was not someone suffering in a private room at a nearby hospital. This was open, exposed, unprotected, painful human suffering. John tells us that Jesus entered into this sea of human need and proceeded to heal one person. *One person.* The obvious question is, why not heal more? Jesus had the divine power to heal everybody, but He chose to heal only one. No doubt, on the way to the one man, Jesus stepped over and around a litany of disabled suffering people. And while it is speculation, I think it's a fair guess that there were thousands begging Him for His healing touch on the way out. They had just seen the Lord Jesus heal. Surely they should be the next in line for a divine touch from the Great Physician.

Here's the compelling question that gave me pause. Later that day, did Jesus feel guilt and remorse for healing only one? Did Jesus slap His forehead and say, "What was I thinking! I just remembered! I'm God. I could have healed everyone. Why didn't I hang out for at least another ten minutes and heal a couple of additional people? Wow, I really regret My actions!" Did Jesus ever think anything close to that? Of course not! Jesus's actions were not driven by opportunity or need. His actions were not dictated by the expectations of others. Jesus was guided solely by the prompting of the Holy Spirit. While we may struggle with regret—Jesus did not.

That hit me hard. All too often, I feel the need to work just a little harder to serve a few more people. Why? Maybe it's a messiah complex. Maybe it's an unquenchable longing to be indispensable to others. Perhaps it's me looking to find my affirmation in the words of others rather than the promise of Jesus. Think of it this way—if Jesus was content doing His Father's will and then calling it a day, and after a full day's work, I cannot call it a day because I feel the compulsion to make one additional phone call, I have a problem! The Son of God could walk away from a need that He could obviously meet, and I cannot! Who do I think I am?

Needs and opportunities confront your pastor every day. And pastors are called to follow the leading of the Holy Spirit every day. Faced with an overwhelming to-do list, countless phone calls to be returned, and long lines of people seeking a meeting with them, pastors need to look to the Holy Spirit to determine which appointment, which call, which task should take priority. This would mean that they would be following the leading of the Holy Spirit and living their lives before an audience of One rather than allowing their schedules to be dictated by the expectations of church members.

At the end of the day, the goal of pastors should be to say with Jesus, "I glorified you on earth, having accomplished the work that you gave me to do" (John 17:4). Jesus surely had not done the work most people expected of Him, but as He lived *coram Deo* (living before the face of God so that His is the only face or opinion that matters), hearing His voice above other internal and external voices, He accomplished what the Father sent Him to do. Sadly, many pastors' schedules are not determined *coram Deo*. They are not protected by capacity. Instead, pastors can be so driven by the approval of others that they go to another local ministry banquet instead of their daughter's Little League game. Because of expectations, pastors attend another evening church board meeting rather than going to the baseball game with the man struggling with his marriage. Even though they may be living a life controlled by the Holy Spirit, when pastors cease to fulfill the expectations of the church, they may be relieved of their pastoral responsibilities. In many ways, pastors are living to please church members rather than living before the only Face that really matters.

Jesus was not driven by opportunity or need. Jesus was wholly directed by the prompting of the Holy Spirit. What would the church look like if pastors committed their daily schedules in prayer, asking for their plans to be determined by the leading of the Holy Spirit? What would it look like to have a moment-by-moment connection that allows your pastor to ask the Holy Spirit what he should do—and then do it? I am not implying that we throw pastoral job descriptions to the wind. I am begging the church to allow their pastor's job description to be limited by their capacity and guided by the Holy Spirit. Allow your pastor to do what the Lord is leading him to do. Allow your pastor to truly live his life *coram Deo*, before an audience of One.

Life Interruptions

Another factor that impacts capacity depth is how one views life's little interruptions. While we can't change the breadth of one's clock capacity, we can impact the depth of one's heart capacity. How many times have you heard someone say, "I just can't get anything accomplished with these constant interruptions!"? How often does someone stick their head into their pastor's office and say, "Sorry to interrupt; I just have a quick question"?

Today I'm writing in my home office. I've been counting, and while writing this short paragraph, I have been interrupted ten times. I received a phone call that I needed to take. I received two texts, one demanding an immediate reply as it came from a pastor in crisis. My daughter had a question about driving her to a volleyball game, my wife had several questions about the kids' schedule, and Murphy, our golden retriever, made it clear he needed a little attention. And you know what? That's life!

Gloria Mark, PhD, associate professor at the Donald Bren School of Information and Computer Sciences at the University of California–Irvine, and a leading expert on work patterns and environments, researched workplace interruptions and came to a fascinating conclusion: "We don't have work days—we have work minutes that last all day." Dr. Mark found that the average amount of time people spent on any single event before being interrupted was three minutes five seconds. Mark went on to say, "What fascinates me is that people interrupted themselves almost as much as they were interrupted by external sources. They interrupted themselves about 44 percent of the time."[1] Translated, in an eight-hour workday, someone working in a typical workplace office environment will be interrupted an average of 160 times per day. It's no less for your pastor. The challenge is that when people are interrupted, they don't immediately go back to the task they were working on before being interrupted.

I remember during my senior year at Wheaton College when I first read C. S. Lewis's thoughts on interruptions. Lewis's perspective changed my life. Since that time (1983), I have referenced Lewis's perspective in any message related to time. In a letter to Arthur Greeves dated December 20, 1943, Lewis writes about Minto, his nickname for his close friend Janie Moore.

> Things are pretty bad here. Minto's varicose ulcer gets worse and worse, domestic help harder and harder to come by. Sometimes I am very unhappy, but less so than I have often been in what were (by external standards) better times. The great thing, if one can, is to stop regarding all the unpleasant things as interruptions of one's "own," or "real" life. The truth is of course that what one calls the interruptions are precisely one's real life—the life God is sending one day by day: what one calls one's "real life" is a phantom of one's own imagination.[2]

As Lewis encourages, our depth of our capacity increases when we understand that the interruptions we experience are not interruptions to life, but rather they are life itself! While you feel frustration because of interruptions, view these interruptions as God's divine appointments orchestrated by the Lord. Jeremiah 10:23 reminds us, "I know, O Lord, that the way of man is not in himself, that it is not in man who walks to direct his steps."

In regard to your pastor, first I encourage you to do everything you can to provide him uninterrupted times of study. This is particularly important as messages are prepared. Second, I encourage you to pray that your pastor would view interruptions as God's divine mini-appointments. Pray that he would find great joy and satisfaction in responding to the many interruptions that will inevitably come his way.

You Can Enlarge Your Pastor's Capacity

You can significantly enlarge your pastor's capacity by fulfilling your role as a follower of Jesus. Ephesians 4:11–16 tells us that the church member carries a responsibility to do the work of the ministry. To the church member Paul writes:

> And he gave the apostles, the prophets, the evangelists, the shepherds and teachers, to equip the saints for the work of ministry, for building up the body of Christ, until we all attain to the unity of the faith and of the knowledge of the Son of God, to mature manhood, to the measure of the stature of the fullness of Christ, so that we may no longer be children, tossed to and fro by the waves and carried about by every wind of doctrine, by human cunning, by craftiness

in deceitful schemes. Rather, speaking the truth in love, we are to grow up in every way into him who is the head, into Christ, from whom the whole body, joined and held together by every joint with which it is equipped, when each part is working properly, makes the body grow so that it builds itself up in love.

Paul reminds believers that the primary role of the pastor is to equip them for the work of ministry. And yet, the average member has abdicated his responsibility to serve as an evangelist in the church to the pastor. As a church member, it is your responsibility to take the message of the gospel to the unbeliever. The only way this will happen is when the casual church member becomes the committed church member.

Pastoral Ministry Is a High Calling

If you are a follower of Jesus, you are called to full-time Christian ministry. It may be full-time medical ministry, full-time educational ministry, or full-time retail ministry. We are each called to serve, understanding that our place of ministry is wherever God has placed us. That said, I do believe that the calling to pastoral ministry is a unique high calling. Don't naively believe that you could run a church more effectively than your pastor because, after all, you're a really smart businessman: "Come on! How hard can it be to serve as a pastor? I've run a successful business. If I can do that—I can most definitely serve as a pastor!" I am troubled when someone disparages the role of the pastor. I am angered when people speak about the

pastoral ministry as a last resort for anyone seeking employment. I
am frustrated when people think they could easily serve in a pastoral
role. I side with the great preacher C. H. Spurgeon, who is reported
to have said, "Let the best and the brightest become pastors. The rest
can become doctors and attorneys."

Remember, your schedule is not your pastor's schedule. Your capacity is different. Most have no idea of the capacity challenges facing
pastors. Love your pastor well. Love by guarding your pastor's capacity!

An Eternal Perspective

Finally, understand that as a follower of Jesus, you will never be at
peace with time. There will always be some measure of tension with
your pastor over his use of time. The reason is simple. We are eternal
beings. And because we are eternal, the Bible reminds us that the
limitation of time is actually evil. Think of time locked in a dungeon,
forced to serve a destructive purpose. We are called daily to break
into the evil dungeon of futility and rescue time, freeing it for God's
redeeming purpose.

> Look carefully then how you walk, not as unwise but
> as wise, making the best use of the time, because the
> days are evil. Therefore do not be foolish, but under-
> stand what the will of the Lord is. (Ephesians 5:15–17)

Scripture refers to the breadth of time as *chronos* and the depth
of time as *kairos*. In Ephesians 5, Paul is speaking of kairos. Most in
this world see time only in terms of chronos. They are obsessed with

chronos and how to get more of it all while failing to see the bigger picture of kairos. In *Walking on Water*, Madeleine L'Engle says:

> Kairos has nothing to do with chronological time. In kairos we are completely unselfconscious, and yet paradoxically far more real than we can ever be when we're constantly checking our watches for chronological time. The artist at work is in kairos. The child at play, totally thrown outside herself in the game, be it building a sand castle or making a daisy chain, is in kairos. In kairos we become what we are called to be as human beings, co-creators with God, touching on the wonder of creation.[3]

We each have a limited number of days on this earth before the Lord Jesus calls us to our eternal home. What needs to be done today to make the best use of the chronos given to you by the Lord? What needs to be done today to make the best use of the kairos moments presented to you by the Lord? Are there letters you need to write? Do you need to make amends with a friend who hurt you? Do you need to spend quality time with your children? Get right with God? Don't begin your day by asking, *How much time do I have and how can I maximize the time I have?* While this is not a bad question, it's a one-dimensional, chronos-only question. Begin each day by asking the Lord Jesus to fully redeem the time He has set before you this day.

Chapter 5

Friendship with Your Pastor
It's Not for Most

Bill led a successful church in the Carolinas. Nestled among the Appalachian Mountains, he and his bride came to the church when he was twenty-eight, originally serving as youth pastor to a small yet growing congregation. At the tender age of thirty-two, Bill was installed as senior pastor and quickly began leading the church to unprecedented growth. An incredibly gifted preacher, Bill attracted many people to the church, some traveling from neighboring cities to listen to his anointed teaching.

When Bill was in his forties, he began writing about church growth, which earned him a spot on the coveted pastor conference speaking circuit. His church was proud that he had become a national leader in the church growth movement. Now in his late forties, Bill was well loved by his congregation, having served the church for twenty-two years. Many within the church longed to be Bill's friend, inviting him to numerous sporting events, concerts, and theatrical events. Some men in the church went further, inviting Bill to accompany them to Montana on fly-fishing trips and even to Africa on hunting expeditions. Bill was experiencing unfathomable new adventures with new friends.

That is, until it was revealed that Bill had incurred debt totaling an astounding three hundred thousand dollars and he was declaring bankruptcy. It was also revealed that Bill had submitted false expense reports in an attempt to secure money to pay his enormous debts. He was immediately fired from his position, and he and his wife were forced to sell their home and move into a small apartment (with their two high school–age children). Before Bill's first paycheck from a new job arrived, the family was forced to go to a local food pantry to ask for bread and soup. The family literally had no money. A local ministry provided a gas card for Bill to allow him to purchase fuel to drive to his job on the midnight shift at UPS.

Tragically, when Bill no longer held the position of senior pastor, the majority of his friends within the church disappeared. I first met Bill three months after he was fired from the church. His congregation asked PastorServe to provide care (do you see the irony?) to their former senior pastor. In my first conversation with Bill, he broke down in tears and asked me, "Do you think any of those men were really my friends, or were they using me because of my position of power within the church?"

Later that week, I accompanied Bill to visit John, the CEO of a local engineering company and his "best friend" in the congregation. I began to inwardly question the depth of the friendship when I learned that Bill and John had not spoken since the firing three months earlier. When we walked into the spacious waiting room, John approached us and asked me into his office without Bill. With little introduction, John abruptly informed me that he resented Bill coming to his office. I shared with John the need for Bill to experience the support of his friends during a time of turmoil, shame, and humiliation. John responded by telling me that he would gladly be Bill's friend—when Bill got his life together. I felt the anger rising within me.

I took a deep breath and measured my words before I responded. "If you refuse to be Bill's friend today and walk with him through the deepest valley of his life, then you were never his friend. You were using Bill because of his position to meet some deep need for power and affirmation in your life. If Jesus treated you the way in which you are treating Bill, no one would be a child of God."

While your pastor will likely never embezzle funds from the church, your pastor can and will sin. And when his sin becomes public, true friends will stand shoulder to shoulder, encouraging, correcting, and loving. Friendship is not for the moment. While the joy of friendship allows us to experience the summits of life with one another, true friendship also means walking with one another through the deep valleys of sin, disappointment, anguish, and unbelief.

Every pastor will encounter the storms of life. Every pastor will go through deep valleys. Every pastor struggles with sin. Pastors need friends—*real friends*—who will walk with them through the storm, through the valley, and through the sin. When people seek friendship with their pastors only to meet an idol of power that lurks within them, they allow idolatry to twist their souls.

Why Pastors Don't Trust People in the Church

Stories like Bill's are common, and as a result, pastors closely guard their hearts, carefully limiting their friendships. Pastors are predisposed to caution when it comes to friendship within the congregation. I remember a man in my congregation who approached me saying that he felt a deep need to confess his deepest sins to his pastor. After taking a good half hour confessing a litany of sins, he looked me in the eyes and said, "Okay, your turn. I've confessed my sins to you; now you confess your sins to me." I assured him that (1) I had a small group of men to whom I confessed my sins, (2) he was not a part of that group, and thus (3) I would not be confessing my sins to him.

Understand that most every pastor at one time or another has been burned by people who have been let in and have misused the information.

The Six Roles in a Pastor's Life

A good friend is just one of the six roles a pastor needs in his life in order to have the best opportunity to thrive in the pastoral ministry. Three of the roles fall on the professional side, and three fall on the personal side. The three professional roles are boss, coach, and trainer. The three personal roles are mentor, counselor, and friend. I (Jimmy) have written extensively about these roles in an earlier book, *Survive or Thrive: Six Relationships Every Pastor Needs*. I would encourage you to purchase a copy for your pastor.

Typically a pastor can identify his **boss**. Nearly every pastor has a board of elders or deacons, a church council, or a geographic governing body overseeing their work while providing structure and accountability. If the pastor is the boss with no structure for accountability, there is almost always trouble on the horizon.

Engaging a **trainer** is a commitment to continuing education. A trainer can be a speaker at a pastor's conference or the pastor of a nearby church. Often a short-term relationship, trainers focus on the process of acquiring pastoral skills. Sadly, the majority of pastors are unable to attend pastor conferences because of finances and/or schedule. And the majority of pastors in America today are bivocational, which means that a pastor's conference hits the pastor in the pocketbook twice—once for the cost of the conference and again with the lost income from their regular job. As a church, commit to provide continuing education for your pastor.

A **coach** will focus on pastoral skills, the pastor's performance, and the task at hand. Coaching is usually a twenty-four-to-thirty-six-month relationship, although a coaching relationship can last for several years. Coaching is peer oriented. Coaching is regular conversations (as opposed to a monologue) that follow a systematic process centered on a defined set of skills, which can be learned and developed and leads to improved and eventually superior performance.

On the personal side, pastors need a **mentor** who focuses on life skills. A mentor will assist the pastor in navigating the labyrinth of life. This is often a lifelong relationship. Many pastors reconnect with a pastor who had a significant impact on their life or a seminary professor who significantly shaped their life.

The most effective pastors have a **counselor**. A coach looks forward, while a counselor looks back, providing personal insight into one's self. The focus is on self-perception and how to cope with interpersonal relationships.

Finally, every pastor needs a **friend or encourager**. The pastor needs close friends who are 100 percent committed to providing encouragement through regular conversation, prayer, and unconditional support.

I can't count the number of times I have met with a pastor who tells me that he heads a staff-led church (which means that *he* is the boss) and he has never had a coach. Furthermore, he doesn't have a trainer because he is the trainer. He goes on to tell me that he lost touch with his mentor fifteen years ago, he has never been to counseling, and if he were 100 percent honest, he doesn't have one single friend.

When I encounter a pastor who has none of the six roles in his life, I know he is ripe for a fall. Pastors must have each of the six roles filled—including the role of friendship. Pastors without friends are pastors teetering on the precipice of destruction.

Serving from the Shadows

Now here is the tough part. Just because your pastor needs friends does not necessarily mean that God has called you to be one of those friends! Because every friendship carries some measure of risk, your pastor may have only a few close friends. And that is okay! You must be willing to serve and pray for your pastor from the shadows. Not everyone in the church will be a best friend to the pastor. If your church has more than two hundred regular attendees, odds are you will not be personal friends with the pastor. If your church is above two thousand, odds are you will never spend personal time with your pastor. And if your church is larger than five thousand, odds are you have never even met your pastor.

If you are reading this book specifically to learn how to become a personal best friend to your pastor—burn the book! This book is not intended to provide you with tools of influence to get into your pastor's personal life. If you want to be good friends with your pastor, check your motives. Why do you want to be such a close friend? Are you like John, whose relationship with Bill was not about friendship but about power?

If you believe you have a calling from the Lord to be a friend to your pastor, but you find that there is resistance, it's okay! Don't take it personally. Remember that most pastors have been burned by people who said they wanted to be their friend. Despite your perceived calling, it may be that God wants you to be an encourager and supporter—but not the friend.

Allow your pastor to maintain boundaries. Despite what you think, there is a limit to what you can or should know about your pastor. Don't expect to learn everything about your pastor's life— that is not your role or your place. Respect other boundaries in the pastor's life. Don't bother the pastor when you see him out with his family. Respect his right to have family time apart from the intrusion of church members. Recently, I was attending my daughter's soccer game when someone approached me and informed me that he was leaving on a mission trip the following week. He went on to tell me (as my daughter scored a goal) that he had been asked to preach and he would like my feedback on his sermon that he had written. Before I could respond, he proceeded to walk through his entire sermon with me. Do you know what that makes him? Insensitive, self-centered, and apparently unaware that pastors have a life. Don't be that guy! There *are* times when pastors are meant to focus solely on their family. Respect your pastor's boundaries.

The most common scenario I hear from pastors goes something like this: "I am struggling to find the balance between my ministry

and my family. I feel an obligation to be at every church staff meeting, leadership meeting, committee meeting, and numerous other
meetings—I feel as if I am out nearly every night. This cheats my
family over and over again." Because of its significance, a statement
I highlighted in chapter 4 is worth repeating here. When asked how
one can balance ministry and family, my response is that the question is framed in the wrong paradigm, because *all of life is ministry
and a pastor's family is his primary ministry*. When your pastor is
absent from the third evening board meeting this week because he's
attending his daughter's soccer game, he is not cheating the church
to be with his family. Rather, he chose his *primary* ministry over his
secondary ministry. He made the right decision! Grant your pastor
the freedom to make his family his primary ministry.

How to Treat Your Pastor as a Friend First and Your Pastor Second

Some of my best conversations on airplanes have ended abruptly
when I am asked about my vocation. There is a part of me that dreads
telling my seatmate that I am a pastor. It's not that I am ashamed of
my calling. In fact, I love my calling to serve as a pastor. It's just that
once the pastor label goes up, the exchange suddenly seems to be
calculated. An additional layer of guarded skepticism is erected and
the conversation feels strained.

I am always looking for ways to be honest yet not immediately
divulge my pastoral role.

"So, what do you do for a living?"

"I'm a coach."

"Oh really? That's awesome. Who do you coach? Are you a sports coach?"

"No, actually, I am a professional coach who helps people perform better in their role."

"Okay, are you coaching business professionals?"

"Actually, I coach pastors."

And that's when the emotional barricade is quickly constructed.

As Larry stressed in chapter 2, pastors want their friends to know them as "Bill," not just the pastor. Don't always introduce your pastor as your pastor. Introduce him as your friend.

If you are out with other friends, do you say, "This is my auto mechanic—auto mechanic Bob; and this is my accountant—accountant Dave"? No! Then why do we do this with our pastors? Allow the fact that your friend is a pastor to emerge naturally in a conversation.

Imagine being a doctor and going to a family gathering where you were asked to conduct a complete physical. (For some of you doctors, this is reality.) Or, what if one by one, every family member lined up and proceeded to describe their symptoms and asked for a diagnosis and a prescription to ease their aches and pains? Similarly, what if the auto mechanic was asked to check the brakes at every gathering he attended? What if the roofer was asked to inspect your roof? Don't think, *Well, since I'm having lunch with my pastor, I should probably ask every deep spiritual question I have ever had.* You don't *always* need to talk about

- spiritual matters;
- personal problems;

- politics (a no-win for the pastor);
- great moral questions of the day; or
- a deep spiritual insight that came to you during your devotions, which the pastor should somehow work into his next sermon.

To be sure, there is a time and place to discuss these topics. And yet, it is vital for you to understand that topics like these can turn a meeting from replenishing into draining. You can talk about sports and other hobbies, and that's okay. What are your pastor's interests? Your pastor may want to talk about his passions—football, model trains, and indie bands. Again, don't misunderstand me; there are times to have deep spiritual conversations with your pastor, but not *every* conversation needs to be a profound spiritual exchange.

Get to know your pastor as a person. What is his story? Where did he come from? Where did he go to school? What are his hobbies? How is he *really* doing? When I talk with pastors and ask them how they are doing, many, before answering the question, tell me through their tears that they are seldom, if ever, asked this question.

On a similar line, don't pigeonhole your pastor. Don't always ask the pastor to pray. Don't ask your pastor, "I have a neighbor who isn't a believer—can you meet with him?" Pastors do not have an answer for every hard question in life. We can't convince every one of your friends to give their life to Jesus. We hold no special line of communication to God. There is so little room or grace given for the pastor to simply say, "I don't know."

Final Thoughts on Friendship with Your Pastor

The number of people who can and should become friends with their pastors is few and far between. If deep friendship happens, it will be in its own time and in its own way. It should not be your goal or your driving force. Caring for your pastor does not always involve being the pastor's friend.

Never forget—your pastor needs God's grace just as much as you do. Are you okay with your pastor's flaws? Are you okay that your pastor is as messed up as you are? Are you okay with the fact that your pastor has doubts and unanswered questions?

Rich is a friend who has served as my contractor for the past fifteen years. He is a skilled worker who has fixed my roof after a hailstorm, installed new countertops in my kitchen, and installed new plumbing in my basement. He has rescued me when I've tried to fix my own electrical problems (not a good idea), and he has fixed destroyed ceilings when a toilet overflowed. When I ask him if he will cut his price if I help, he always responds, "If you insist on helping, I will charge you double." Rich is more than my contractor. He has become a friend.

One night I decided to drive to his home to drop off a check for some work he had done. When I pulled up to Rich's house, I was a bit shocked! The front door was broken. Paint was peeling from the house. The porch light was broken, and I had to pound on the front door once I realized the doorbell wasn't working. When Rich answered the door, I laughed and said, "I know a good contractor if you want to get this place fixed up."

How many pastors are similar to my contractor? They spend countless hours serving your family. They answer your questions, they provide counsel about your marriage difficulties, and they help you through your crisis. Yet, there may be little energy at the end of the day to serve their own family. They may not have the strength to dive into their own marital challenges. I have heard many pastors' spouses say, "You fix everyone else's marriage; why can't you fix ours?"

Create space for your pastor to be a real person. Be a friend—either personally or in the shadows—but be a friend to your pastor. Give him the opportunity to repair his own house as he has repaired the homes of so many others.

Every Pastor Needs a Bob

It was as if I had died and gone to heaven. Bob, one of the elders in our church, had invited me to attend a Celtics playoff game—against the hated New York Knicks at the old Boston Garden. Needless to say, I jumped at the opportunity!

Although it was many years ago, the night sticks in my mind as if it were yesterday. To say Bob was a wonderfully out-of-control Celtics fan would be a massive understatement. Hubie Brown was the coach of the Knicks. We took our seats and the game was no more than a couple of minutes old when Bob stood up and screamed at the top of his lungs, "Hey, Hubie, you suck!"

Do you have any idea how awesome that was? It was clear that Bob was not going to play the game of impressing his pastor with his deep spirituality. He was not going to hold back because he was with his pastor. He was a real guy with real passions, and while he was glad I was along, he was not going to put on a show for anyone. That night, Bob never once introduced me as a pastor. Throughout the evening, I was his friend.

Pastors need friends like Bob. Sadly, all too often, pastors and isolation go hand in hand. Pastoring is lonely. A majority of pastors report that they walk though life alone without a single friend.

And yet, there is something deeper. Why does this strike such a profound chord? Because it reminds us that ultimately our true friend is Jesus. It reminds us of the gospel. The good news of the gospel is that Jesus Christ came to earth so we would never walk alone. Proverbs 18:24 reminds us that there is a friend who sticks closer than a brother. Hebrews 13:5 promises us that Christ will never leave us. Indeed, because of Jesus, we never walk alone. When you are a friend to your pastor, you are the visible hands and feet of Jesus.

Chapter 6

Pastoral Compensation
Reflecting God's Generosity

After many years of education, two internships, and a pastoral residency, Kenny and Mary were excited to finally begin their church-planting adventure. A young, energetic couple, they were relieved that they would need to endure just one final meeting before being officially approved to move to the city where they would launch the new work. As the lengthy three-month assessment process drew to a close, they met with their denominational committee. At this point, approval was an apparent formality, but final questions had to be asked, boxes checked, and forms signed. As the meeting wrapped up, one member of the committee commented on how pleased the denomination was that the couple would be entering into church planting with no debt. It was a blessing to the denomination to see a young couple begin a new church without a dark financial cloud hanging over their head. Kenny proudly responded, "By God's grace, and through a great deal of discipline, we have no debt. We have yet to purchase our first home, our car is paid in full, and we have zero credit card debt." The committee was clearly pleased.

One member said, "Well, that is great to hear. It's quite an accomplishment to have no auto loans, no credit card debt, and no school loans."

"Oh," the young man responded. "We didn't think about our school loans. *We didn't know that school loans counted as debt.* I guess our data form is incorrect."

"Well," asked the committee member, "how much do you owe on your school loans?"

"Do you mean each one of us or all together?" Kenny asked.

"How much *combined* school debt do you have *all together?*" a committee member patiently asked.

"Eighty-five thousand dollars" was the sheepish response. The committee sat in stunned silence.

Sadly, this young pastoral couple is not unlike countless others who serve in pastoral ministry. Pastors all too often begin their pastoral journeys under the ominous burden of financial debt, many carrying hefty school loans. Pastors regularly enter into their first pastoral calling struggling to meet monthly financial obligations, unsure how to construct a budget, unable to maintain an expected lifestyle consistent with their churches, and … *embarrassed.* "How did we get into this situation?" *Financial challenges are a major contributing factor to nearly half of the pastors who enter into the ministry and leave between years two and four.* And beyond the initial shock of the financial realities of pastoral ministry, several middle-age pastors depart when they realize that there is zero hope for retirement. Generally speaking, the financial care of pastors is one of the black marks on the church today. Thank God that He doesn't deal with His children in the same manner in which we care for the shepherds who lead our local congregations. The Lord deals with us with extravagant generosity, while some churches honestly believe it is their responsibility to keep their pastors humble by paying them poorly. In this chapter, I will highlight nine practical steps you can take to care for your pastor's financial needs.

Professional Financial Counsel

First, provide your pastor with sound professional financial counsel. Few Bible colleges and seminaries teach the basics of personal financial management. As a teenager, I saw a pastor have a nervous breakdown and a church nearly collapse because of questionable financial decisions. In that moment, knowing I was unquestionably called to the pastoral ministry, I vowed not to be a pastor who knew the Bible and yet didn't understand financial basics. While finishing my education at Wheaton College, I began to take financial management courses at a local Chicago community college. I took classes in real estate, insurance, stocks and bonds, and financial planning. I obtained a Series 6 and 63 security license at the tender age of twenty-two. At the age of twenty-four I began teaching basic financial classes to seminary students (I too was a seminary student at this time). I will never forget some of the most basic of questions that regularly were asked. Some students, who had obviously been under the wing of their parents for a long time, had never opened a checking account. Some had no idea how to file a tax return. One young pastor-in-training asked me if he should stop buying and, in fact, begin selling his high-end stereo equipment. When I inquired as to why he was considering selling his stereo equipment, he responded, "Because I can't afford to buy my daughters shoes." Yes, that is a true story.

Pastors need professional financial counsel. They need a clergy tax specialist to help them with their taxes. They need to be given guidance regarding maximizing the clergy housing allowance (many use only a portion of their housing allowance, thus wasting one of the greatest financial benefits afforded to pastors). They need to be connected with a certified financial planner (I recommend Kingdom Advisors—www.kingdomadvisors.org, an excellent resource to locate a Christian financial advisor). Pastors need a will (which a fraction of pastors have) drawn up by an attorney. A certified professional financial planner will help your pastor create a budget and establish a game plan, because you can't reach a destination without a road map.

One middle-age pastor was shocked to receive a notice in the mail informing him that he owed nearly seventy-five thousand dollars in back taxes. He believed this to be an IRS mistake and fought it with great passion. And yet, it was soon revealed that while he was convinced he had opted out of social security, he had in fact never filed the necessary forms. For several decades, he had not paid social security taxes (FICA), believing he was exempt. The oversight led to him resigning his church and taking a job with a local insurance agency because there was no way to recover from the financial hole and remain in the pastoral ministry being paid an insufficient salary. As he looked back on his financial collapse, he admitted that he knew he needed financial assistance but that he could never afford to have an accountant prepare his tax return or a financial advisor to review his financial situation, either of which would have likely revealed the IRS oversight.

The Pastor's Salary? Be Generous

Second, be generous when establishing your pastor's salary. Far too many churches tell me that they want to be fair when setting their pastors' salaries. Fair generally means that the church wants to pay no more than the market rate for their pastor. Why do we bring a scarcity mentality to the table when it comes to our pastors? When setting your pastor's salary, I encourage you to go beyond fair and be generous.

I can assure you, your pastor did not enter the ministry to get rich. He was well aware of the financial sacrifice entering the ministry would demand. But neither do pastors enter the ministry expecting to live a life characterized by debt and constant financial shortfall. Measure by any standard you desire (education, hours per week, gifting), your pastor is well worth the generous salary he should be paid.

Practically speaking, you need to pay your pastor a wage that will allow him to live in the community in which he is called to minister. I know of a young man who was hired as a youth pastor at a large suburban church. It was made clear that he was expected to live in the middle of the community where 90 percent of the students attended high school. And yet, as the youth pastor, he was paid a ridiculously low salary. He and his wife looked for an apartment and found that they were priced out of the local community. They began to put offers on low-end decrepit fixer-upper houses. Incredibly, nearly a dozen offers later, they still weren't able to move into the community. They began expanding their search area. Several *months* later they finally found an apartment in their price range, thirty-seven miles away from the church! Do you think the church raised the pastor's salary to compensate for excessive mileage? Not on your life. No other pastor was given a mileage compensation in their salary; why should he? Four years and tens of thousands of miles later, the youth pastor took a position in another church that paid a salary allowing him to live fewer than two miles from the church.

I know of one church who took 1 Timothy 5:17–18 to heart. Believing the admonition to provide "double honor" to those who teach in the church, the elders averaged their income and then doubled that figure to set the pastor's salary! While they were criticized by some, they agreed if they were to err, they would err on the side of radical generosity. May their tribe increase!

The Scriptures paint a picture of an elaborately generous God. God *generously* gives us wisdom (James 1:5); God grants us life *abundantly* (John 10:10); He fills our cup until it *overflows* (Psalm 23:5); He *generously* gives good gifts to His children (Matthew 7:11); God's mercy is *abundant* (Psalm 51:1). This is not a picture of a scarcity-mentality God. This is a picture of plentiful generosity from an abundantly kind heavenly Father.

I have heard some set forth the argument that the church is called to give pastors what they need—and nothing more. To give an abundance would be poor stewardship. There are two different stories detailing a miraculous catch of fish by Jesus's disciples (Luke 5; John 21). How many fish did the disciples need? In Luke 5, we are told that the number of fish was so great that their nets began to break. When they called their buddies to help, they filled both boats so full that they both began to sink. Again I will ask—how many fish did they need? How many fish did Jesus provide? Jesus abundantly, lavishly provided.

When I stand before the throne of God the Father Almighty, the last thing I am going to mention is fairness. And trust me, I want nothing to do with justice. I need unmerited mercy and undeserved generosity. *When we are generous with our pastors, we are dimly reflecting the generosity that the Lord has graciously extended to us.* Before you set your pastor's salary, read Ephesians 1:3–8, which reminds us that God the Father has blessed us with *every* spiritual blessing and that we have redemption through the *riches* of His grace, which He *lavished* on us. God wasn't fair when He accomplished our redemption. Rather, He was deeply generous, profusely pouring the treasure of His grace on us.

Pastoral Benefits

Third, be proactive when considering pastoral benefits. Far too often, pastoral benefits are *reactive* rather than *proactive*. The church offers a sabbatical when they recognize their pastor is near burnout. Personal counseling is offered when the pastor shows signs of anxiety. Marriage counseling is encouraged after relational cracks become visible, resulting in the pastor being sent to SonScape Retreats (always a good idea—but it's better if you're proactive). A gym membership is purchased for the staff when one of the pastors suffers a mild heart attack. An EAP (Employee Assistance Program, such as PastorCare offers through PastorServe) is made a standard part of the staff package when the staff begins to show signs of emotional fatigue. Continuing education becomes the standard only after the pastoral staff confesses an inability to lead in the area of stewardship. A book allowance is included in pastoral packages only when it is revealed that the pastoral staff has not read an intellectually stimulating book in the past year because they can't afford to purchase books on their salary. *Don't wait for the crisis to hit before providing benefits to address the issues that most pastors will inevitably face!*

Do not be the church that argues, "We would love to proactively provide additional pastoral benefits, but we simply can't afford the cost." In reality, you may be surprised to learn that caring for your pastor *proactively* will ultimately *save* the church money. The average cost of replacing a pastor is one and a half times the salary of the pastor. By caring for the pastor now, you will create a culture of care that pastors will appreciate, and that will encourage them to stay!

One church balked at spending an additional seventy-five hundred dollars a year to care for their lead pastor, which ultimately contributed to his departure. They felt as though they couldn't afford an EAP, a proactive marriage intensive, or a gym membership. And yet, upon his departure, they paid a severance package, hired a search firm to fill the lead pastor role, and gave the new pastor a generous moving package. The total cost of the change in leadership was more than *fifty times* what they had refused to proactively spend to care for their pastor! Have a long-range perspective! Proactively care for your pastor! It will cost you *less* to care now (before the bumps in the road—*which always come*) rather than later.

Be generous when considering pastoral benefits. Give consideration to excellent health insurance (include dental), an EAP, a gym membership, and a book allowance. Send your pastors to SonScape Retreats once every three years (reminder: this is Jimmy writing this—not Larry!). Provide laptops or tablets, and pay for their mobile phones. The majority of pastors have woefully inadequate life insurance. Provide a minimum of two and a half years of annual salary of term life insurance.

I commonly hear the lay leadership of the church respond to my suggestions by saying, "A sabbatical *and* generous benefits? That

seems overly generous. I don't get benefits like this at *my* workplace."
My response: "Why do you consider your workplace the standard?
Shouldn't the church be the place where we most clearly model the
standard of employee care that we want the world to reflect?" I dream
of the church treating their pastors in such a way that one day the
business world will say, "Wow! Seriously? That's a benefit at this
company? That is over the top! My church doesn't even do that for
our pastors."

Pastoral Expense Account

Fourth, provide your pastor with an expense account. All too often,
a pastor is paid a substandard wage and then is expected to cover
the majority of his regular pastoral expenses. While most churches
understand covering costs relating to conference and denominational
travel, few understand the day-to-day expenses incurred by pastors in
the course of a normal day. Taking a leader out to lunch, providing
the meal for the small group leaders at their home, and driving to
visit a shut-in at a retirement home forty miles from the church—it
all adds up. I know many pastors who regularly spend close to five
hundred dollars per month out of their own pocket with no anticipa-
tion of reimbursement, and this is without mileage—which would in
many cases be another five hundred out of pocket. When a pastor is
paid a minimal wage, and then is expected to cover mileage, phone,
and most expenses, it is a financial black hole. I know that many if
not most pastors are in this situation, and I also know that many if
not most feel immensely uncomfortable bringing this up. Pastors
do not want to take their board members out to Ruth's Chris steak

house for lunch. But neither do they want to have every leadership meeting meal at Costco. Know that this is an uncomfortable topic. Have a heart-to-heart discussion with your pastor. Be generous! That would be a huge step in the right direction.

Establish a Sabbatical Policy

Fifth, related to financial generosity, have a sabbatical policy in place. The majority of pastors, despite having a day off, are on call 24-7. I can recount dozens and dozens of stories of pastors interrupting family vacations to return to their home church to lead a funeral or deal with a crisis. Pastors need a sabbatical when they know they will not be called.

A sabbatical is rooted in the biblical concept of "Sabbath," which God modeled (Genesis 2:2–3) and commanded (Exodus 20:8–11). In Leviticus 25:1–7, the Lord commanded that after the sixth year the people were not supposed to sow the fields or harvest a crop. The land was allowed to rest and, therefore, so were the people. Sabbaticals are not extended vacations, but an extended period of time devoted to study, reflection, rest, recovery, and renewal.

A sabbatical is most often granted after seven years of full-time service in a single local church. Some churches operate on the model of pastors being eligible for a three-month sabbatical after five years of ministry or a six-month sabbatical after seven years of service. The pastor needs to submit a well-planned, detailed sabbatical schedule and goals to church leadership a minimum of three months prior to departure. The best sabbaticals will be enthusiastically supported by the church. Any sabbatical should include rest, a family vacation, an opportunity to visit other churches, and planned objectives (I want to grow in my understanding of worship). During a sabbatical, the pastor is 100 percent removed from day-to-day life of the church. Contact with the pastor (aside from regular reports) is only in case of emergency. The pastor attends churches other than his own.

A sabbatical is important to both the pastor and the church. It reminds the church that any one pastor is not the key to the church. Pastors can become idols, and sabbaticals remind the congregation that their worth as a church is founded in Jesus Christ, not the particular giftings of their pastor.

I recently met with a pastor who told me about his recent sabbatical. He was able to take a long overdue family vacation, read a number of books, and visit three churches. When I inquired regarding the length of his sabbatical, he told me the church had granted him six weeks. Please understand this—*there is no such thing as a six-week sabbatical!* Six weeks away is nothing but an extended vacation! For any pastor (but particularly a lead pastor), it takes a minimum of two weeks to unwind from the intense pressure of day-to-day ministry. As a pastor, you don't just punch out and walk away. It requires time to come down from the emotional rigors of pastoral ministry. In fact, during the first ten days of a sabbatical, it is not unusual for the pastor to be ill, spending most of the time in bed. Why? Because his body lets its guard down, making him more susceptible to illness. Furthermore, two weeks before returning to the church, the pastor is thinking about the congregation, staff, messages to be preached, and next steps to be taken. Whatever length of time you grant to your pastor as a sabbatical, subtract one month and that is the true length of the sabbatical—hence, *there are no six-week sabbaticals.* The ideal

length of a sabbatical is six months. Nine months is even better. The
absolute minimum is three months. Anything less than three months
is not a sabbatical but an extended vacation.

There are numerous important considerations surrounding a sabbatical. For example, we have seen churches struggle mightily when
a lead pastor returns from an extended sabbatical. If other pastors
are allowed to step up and lead during another pastor's sabbatical,
it will likely not go well when the lead pastor returns and staff are
expected to immediately return to their presabbatical responsibilities. Additionally, there are financial considerations. For an extensive
sabbatical discussion, resources, and suggested detailed plans, go to
www.pastorserve.org/sabbatical.

I worked with an upper Midwest church going through serious
issues with their lead pastor and experienced this heartbreaking story.
The pastor's marriage was in shambles, and he was desperately in need
of a break to address these issues with his wife. The church leadership asked me to advise them on working through the difficulties
with the pastor. When I began asking questions, I soon learned
that this pastor had served his congregation for twenty-two years
with no sabbaticals, taking only an average of three weeks vacation
(including study leave) each year. I also learned that he was a hard
worker—regularly putting in an unhealthy sixty-plus hours per
week. During his years at the church, he had taken a grand total of
five vacations with his family, the longest being six days. Most of his
vacation time had been spent leading church mission trips or doing
long-range message preparation.

My recommendation was to immediately grant the pastor a three-
month sabbatical to focus exclusively on his marriage. I encouraged

the church to pay for all counseling and all expenses and to provide a vacation for him and his wife at the conclusion of the three months. When the leadership began to push back, I changed my *recommendation* to an *admonition*. I vehemently assured them that the church *owed* this to their pastor. Twenty-two years of continual service and long weeks with little to no vacation had "earned" him this time to focus on his marriage.

It breaks my heart to say that the leadership of the church could not wrap their minds around a pastor who had issues in his marriage. Nor could they conceive of providing a sabbatical for their pastor. "My workplace would never do this for me" were the exact words spoken. And so they fired their pastor. Twenty-two years of service! Their pastor had walked with nearly every member of the leadership team through their crises, and yet when the pastor encountered personal struggles, they let him go. I cried as I drove to my hotel that night.

Establish a Vacation Policy Separate from Study Leave

Sixth, allow your lead pastor to take a minimum of two weeks a year away from the church for study leave. It takes concentrated time to evaluate the direction of the church, construct sermon series, create sermon outlines, and plan an annual calendar. All too often, study leave is included in a pastor's annual vacation. To include study leave as part of a pastor's annual vacation forces the pastor to choose whether he is going to cheat his family or cheat the church. Don't make him make that choice. Additionally, I encourage pastors to take one day away each month for a concentrated time of prayer and meditation.

In the role of lead pastor, provide a minimum of four weeks for vacation, a minimum of two weeks for study leave, and a minimum of twelve days for personal spiritual retreats. Your pastor will be better prepared to teach, lead, serve, and minister.

Don't Be a Cheapskate!

Seventh, don't financially patronize your pastor. I remember pouring close to thirty hours of counseling into a young New England couple. They were preparing to be married and they couldn't have been more excited as they considered their future together, even though they were bringing a great deal of emotional baggage into the marriage. I met with the husband-to-be one on one a number of times, as well as meeting with the couple eight times. The bride-to-be assured me that her father was well aware of the time I was spending with the young couple, and at the right time, he would make sure that I was fairly compensated.

Weddings and funerals can be a nice opportunity for your pastor to make some additional income that is often a huge blessing. I know of many family vacations that were funded by weddings and funerals. "Thank God Mrs. Hicks died—we're going to Disney World!" Okay, that was a joke! I've never heard those *exact* words.

When providing a gift to your pastor, consider that premarital counseling frequently occurs in the evenings, taking the pastor away from his own family. Remember that a wedding weekend generally consists of a Friday evening rehearsal and a Saturday wedding, taking the pastor away from his own family for the entire weekend. A Golden Corral gift card is not adequate to say thank you. Be generous when thanking your pastor with a financial gift.

The rehearsal dinner for the New England couple was the most extravagant I had ever witnessed. The father of the bride (who I learned was the CEO of a Fortune 500 company) had not just rented out a country club, but had in fact rented out the entire golf course. Tables had been placed on the eighteenth fairway to accommodate the more than one hundred guests (again, this is the rehearsal dinner!). I can't imagine the money spent to make the evening memorable for everyone, particularly the bride and groom. The following day, I was in the back hallway of the church preparing for the ceremony when the father approached me. He looked around as if he wanted to make sure no one was watching, and then, with a twinkle in his eye, he said these exact words: "Pastor, I am going to grease your palm." Remember, this is the CEO of a Fortune 500 company. I thought it might be plane tickets to Hawaii or a check for five thousand dollars. He then proceeded to place something into my hand. I looked down and saw that he had given me a fifty-dollar bill! Again, I so wish I was making this up to make a point, but this is a true story! I was speechless.

Don't misunderstand; I was grateful for the fifty dollars. In many parts of the world, this would be a month's salary. However, in this case, this averaged out to less than one dollar an hour when you considered the time I had spent doing premarital counseling, the time I'd counseled with the husband, the rehearsal, and the ceremony. What made it worse was in the midst of this ostentatious display, he was being cheap. Perhaps he was being naive—maybe he honestly believed I had never seen a fifty-dollar bill—but I think he was undervaluing my services. I had spent more than fifty dollars in gas driving to the many counseling appointments, rehearsal dinner, and wedding.

When you have an opportunity to financially bless your pastor—*financially bless your pastor*! Don't patronize your pastor. Be generous!

Pastoral Retirement

Eighth, help your pastor build a retirement fund. Many older pastors have no retirement, no assets, and no plan, and they are scared to death. Understand this: the majority of pastors share the same financial plan—*because retirement is not in the Bible* (true, it isn't). And this is the plan: *I will work until I die—and if I go before my spouse, I hope the church will be kind.*

That is wishful thinking, and far from a workable financial strategy. The truth is that most pastors will not pull a V. Raymond Edman, the fourth president of Wheaton College who died in the pulpit in 1967 while preaching the message "In the Presence of the King." That's just not the way it generally works. Most pastors will be forced into retirement by their congregation.

There is intense job *insecurity* in many churches. The lack of a retirement account can and often does lead to risk aversion among older pastors in the local church. Many pastors back away from risk when they are in their fifties and sixties because there is a fear that if they take a risk and fail—one, they may be released; and two, there are few jobs available to a person of their age. While you may have never put the two together, providing your pastor a retirement account will give your pastor the freedom to fail.

The fact is that pastors are poor savers. Most find tremendous joy in being generous, and they live on the edge of a financial cliff. Few pastors in their twenties and thirties have considered the long-term necessity of savings, believing the time to save will start later in life. The church needs to help young pastors begin saving *now*. This is particularly true if your pastor opted out of social security. Because of the benefits of compound interest, beginning a savings program at the age of twenty-two as opposed to thirty-seven could mean the difference of hundreds of thousands of dollars at retirement.

Provide your pastoral staff matching funds for retirement. Give them every available incentive to save. Help your pastor establish and annually fund an IRA. If your pastor opted out of social security, provide the funds you would have paid in the form of a retirement benefit.

Care for the Entire Pastoral Team

Ninth, care for the entire pastoral staff. Too often in a large church, the lion's share of the "pastoral perks" are given to the guy up front. As one who regularly preached at a megachurch for ten years, I understand the benefits that came my way (vacations, tickets, etc.) and yet were never offered to any other member of the pastoral staff. The result is (often) the lead pastor's bucket filled to the brim while the other staff members' buckets are empty. Don't offer your vacation home just to the lead pastor. Offer the home to every member of the pastoral team. Do you have incredible tickets to the playoff game and you want to take a pastor? Great! Invite the associate. It may be that he seldom attends sporting events although he is the biggest sports enthusiast on the staff.

One spectacularly generous family extended an offer to me that I will never forget. I was a guest preacher in their Georgia church. They knew I spent a great deal of time on the road, and after a morning message, they offered to send my family to a resort for seven days of family fun. When I considered the invitation, my heart jumped at the generous offer. My family was in need of a vacation, and it was not a part of our family budget. And yet, the week before, I had spent significant time with several members of the staff, many of whom were burned out and desperately in need of a vacation to recharge their batteries. I knew that for many of the pastors, a seven-day family vacation was an unachievable dream. I asked the couple if they would allow me to take the seven nights they had offered me and find a couple of pastors at the church who needed a break, and give each a three- or four-night family vacation. They told me that they would pray about it and get back to me. They called the next day with a decision that still gives me goose bumps. They said, "We have prayed about this, and here is what we decided. We still want you and Sally to take your family and go away. And, in addition to this, we will give you an additional *forty-nine nights* that you can distribute to the staff as you believe would be helpful!" Wow! More than ten families at that church were able to get away. Some took two nights away sans children, while others took a week to vacation with their family. That gift blessed the entire church more than this couple will ever know!

I understand why it is fun to offer a gift to certain individuals. Let's be honest—it's cool to have your lead pastor or a well-known national figure stay in your beach vacation home. It's not as sexy to have the assistant youth pastor resident intern stay in your vacation home. But *both* need your generosity! While this is not the book to address the underlying issue of the tendency to care exclusively for the lead pastor, a main reason is our propensity to be drawn to the idol of power. We like being friends with well-known leaders. It strokes our ego when the pastor greets us by name. *Be careful not to be sucked in by the idol of power.*

When it comes to pastoral perks, special benefits, or year-end appreciation gifts, remember the entire pastoral staff!

Sadly, I could fill volumes with stories of pastors who have personally suffered because of a lack of generosity from their local church. Conversely, I could count on one hand the stories of over-excessive generosity. Take care of your pastoral team. Be generous. Your pastor will be the first in line to provide help and the last in line to receive help. Know that the pastor and the pastoral team have gone to great lengths to care for you. Go to great lengths to care for them.

Chapter 7

The Pastor's Spouse
Life in a Minefield

If you value your pastor's spouse and family, you will greatly bless your pastor! Ignore your pastor's family and every other thing you do for your pastor will be marginalized. No single element of pastoral care is as significant as loving your pastor's wife and family!

"I will never trust anyone in the church again! Never!" Tears rolled down the cheeks of Beth as she told her story. It had been a hard year of ministry for Roger and Beth. Several families had left the church when Roger let the youth director go because of inappropriate behavior. In the end the whole situation had blown up in Roger's face.

In addition, Roger and Beth's personal finances were in bad shape and their debt was growing. Their son had a rotten attitude, fueled by his poor choices in friends. And their marriage was at an all-time low. A friend recommended a marriage counselor, and Roger and Beth had recently begun weekly sessions.

With family and close friends far away, Beth was overwhelmed and lonely. On a particularly bleak day, Beth had shared her struggles with a woman from the church she thought she could trust. Sharing lightened the load a bit and made her feel a little better.

When she encountered the woman at church the next Sunday, her response seemed cold. In fact, everything felt different at church that day. Beth couldn't put her finger on what it was, at least not until Roger came home from an elder board meeting the next night. The board had found out they were in counseling and had grilled Roger about it. They did not want a pastor who needed counseling. It was the beginning of the end of their ministry at the church.

Six months later they were packing up their possessions with no place to go. If they were ever called to serve a church again, Beth was sure of one thing: *No matter how difficult their circumstances, she would never again open her heart to a church member. Never!*

When she finished sharing her story, Roger reached for her hand. His tears began to flow as he said, "Beth is the most caring and compassionate person I know, but she has shut down. I want my wife back, but I don't know what to do!"

When a pastor is attacked, it hurts. But when he watches his wife or children suffer at the hands of people who call themselves Christians, it is devastating. You cannot truly care for your pastor unless you care for your pastor's spouse and children. If you want to have a profound impact on your pastor, extend a hand to the family.

The Most Difficult Role in the Church

Surprisingly, it is not the role of pastor that is the most difficult, but the role of pastor's wife. Understanding some of the challenges specific to being the wife of a pastor is a necessary part of being an encourager. What you do and why you do it will be effective only as it flows from true understanding.

Before I am accused of sexism, let me say that the role of pastor's wife is very different from the role of pastor's husband. Lumping them both together would be unfair and inaccurate. Near the end of this chapter the uniqueness of the pastor's husband will be addressed. But I will begin with the singular and difficult role of the pastor's wife.

The role of wife has radically changed over the last few decades. If you love early television shows like *Father Knows Best* and *Leave It to Beaver*, you've seen idealized depictions of wives that were popular after the Second World War. Wow! Have things changed over the last sixty years! If I were to suggest to my wife, Barbara, that she should put on a dress and pearls in order to clean the house, I would be sleeping on the sofa—or maybe in the garage.

But I am not so sure much has changed for the pastor's wife. Consider this list based on conversations with hundreds of pastors' wives:

- Do what needs to be done. Stand quietly at your husband's side. Fill in wherever there is a need. Always do more than your share. Never expect thanks or remuneration.

- Prepare yourself. Look good but not too good. Wear makeup, but don't overdo it. If you have any questions, ask the elders' wives and they will instruct you.

- Keep your house in perfect condition (especially if you live in a parsonage). You never know when church members might stop by, and you want the house ready to receive them. Make sure you have coffee and fresh-baked cookies available.

- Prepare your children. Make sure your children are clean, well dressed, and above all, polite. They should never be loud or run in the church. Remember they are the pastor's kids and should always be an example.

- Listen to people. You may have things to say, but your things are not as important as everyone else's. No matter how long or boring the story, smile, smile, smile.

- Never complain. No matter what they say about your husband, your kids, or about you, just take it. No matter how ridiculous their expectations, work to satisfy them. No matter how deeply or unfairly you have been hurt, endure it with joy.

- Make everyone comfortable. From the youngest to the oldest, you are to know them, serve them, and be available to them. Be as good as or better than the former pastor's wife.

- Remember, a good pastor's wife always knows her place.

Sound ridiculous? Talk to your pastor's wife, and you will find out it is not as ridiculous as you might think. When a church hires a pastor, there are written as well as unwritten expectations that go along with the job. A pastor's wife is not hired, so there is no written job description. But in most cases the unwritten expectations are long and often unreasonable. Certainly this is not true for every church nor for every pastor's wife, but there are far too many who have been subjected to absurd standards like those listed above.

Caring for your pastor means caring for your pastor's wife and children. Before you can attend to your pastor's wife, you need to understand her challenging, demanding role.

Living in a Minefield

Larry Crabb wrote a book with a great title—*The Safest Place on Earth*. That is what the church should be. For many pastors' wives it is anything but a safe place. In fact, it seems more like a minefield where every step must be carefully navigated. These wives carry shrapnel from previous missteps along the way. They become extremely cautious and even fearful in their interactions with the people of the church.

Sharing something with a church member, as in Beth's story, is only one of the many potential bombshells of which a pastor's wife must beware. *Whom can I trust? What can I share? Where do I go with my pain and wounds?*

Over and over again, Barbara and I have listened to the deep pain and despair that engulf a pastor's wife as she tries to fulfill a role she never bargained for. Over time what she's endured leads to bitterness. Let me suggest three of the most damaging issues hidden in the minefield that confronts a pastor's wife.

Minefield #1: Expectations

Yes, we're back to expectations. The damage they do to your pastor is equaled by the damage they inflict on your pastor's wife. Reasonable and unreasonable, spoken and unspoken—people's expectations threaten the personality and the passion God instilled within your pastor's wife.

The minefield of people's expectations is huge and dangerous. Those expectations, like the ones that impact their husbands, have similar preconceptions:

- the previous pastor's wife
- the person's own imagination
- a book someone once read
- someone else's thoughts, once shared in a group

Often those expectations are neither right nor fair. But they are very real and they are very dangerous.

Like their husbands, pastors' wives are all different. Not all majored in music in college, nor are all supremely gifted with children. Typing the bulletin or functioning as church secretary does not lie in the comfort zone of every pastor's wife. They do have a wide range of talents, gifts, and dreams, though. Some are the life of the party, while others avoid parties. There are those who have natural abilities as homemakers, while others struggle. Some have great taste in fashion and design, while others have no idea what colors go together, nor do they care. Many have deep faith, but there are others who wrestle with their faith. There are those who pray beautifully in public, while others pray only in private, and some even struggle with their prayer life altogether. Each pastor's wife is uniquely crafted by a loving, wise God. Yet they are all imperfect, damaged by their own sin, and living life in a fallen world. One thing they share in common: they all face expectations from the people who sit in their church every Sunday.

What is your pastor's wife like? What makes her heart come alive? Do you have expectations of her that are outside of her talents and desires? Does the rest of the congregation? Is she expected to be a counselor for the women of the church? What if that's not something she is comfortable with? What if she doesn't want to lead Bible studies for women? Is it acceptable for a pastor's wife to be introverted, avoiding the spotlight? Can she be who God created her to be?

Not all pastors' wives see the church as their primary or even their secondary ministry. (As we have said and will continue to say, their family is their primary ministry.) Some may love teaching in a school or working in the medical field. There are those who are entrepreneurs and business owners. Some love to be at home raising children. They are living out their faith and witness in the places they work or in places they volunteer. That should not only be okay—it should be honored.

Some pastors' wives just want to be left alone! Maybe they have been wounded in the past. Maybe they are working through their own issues in life. Perhaps they are just quiet individuals who want to live in deep intimacy with their Lord and with their loved ones.

So with that understanding, how can you help your pastor's wife in the minefield of expectations?

1. **Examine your own expectations of your pastor's wife.** Get rid of expectations that are unrealistic or just plain wrong.

2. **Let your pastor's wife know she is not hired staff and that you want her to be free to be who she is.** Honor and appreciate her as a unique and beautiful individual. Give her freedom and space.

3. **Stand against unrealistic expectations within the church.** When people express crazy, unrealistic things, challenge them and set them straight. Stand up for your pastor's wife.

Minefield #2: Criticism

Criticism is never easy, but when it comes at those we love most dearly, it is particularly painful. Pastors' wives often watch their spouses serve so faithfully and give so sacrificially only to receive one blow of criticism after another.

"I found my husband sitting on a bench in a park not far from the church. He was only a shell of the man I married. I watched his passion drain from his body as criticism rained down on him blow after blow. He had made mistakes, but he had tried ... he had really tried. I was so sad and I was so angry. But I did not know what to do." Those were the words of one pastor's wife who came to a SonScape retreat, but they reflect the words of so many others.

John 15:12–13 records some of the last words of Jesus to His disciples, *"My command is this: Love each other as I have loved you. Greater love has no one than this: to lay down one's life for one's friends"* (NIV).

Too many pastors' wives have seen anything but a church reflecting love toward its pastor. Their husbands give and give—often more than they should. Frankly, it often creates a dilemma for their wives. They are frustrated and angry at their husbands for giving too much to the church (and not enough to their families), while they hurt deeply for what they watch their husbands endure. On one hand they want to slap their husbands, and on the other hand they want to defend their husbands and slap the church.

"It is not right and it is not fair! I am angry at the church and I am angry at God!" Those are the honest feelings of just one pastor's wife. *Many* echo this sentiment. More than anyone else the wife is aware of her husband's weaknesses. But she also sees her husband's heart. She wonders why no one ever stands up to defend her husband. When she tries, her words are discounted, because she is, after all, only the pastor's wife.

Sometimes unintentionally, their husbands can add to the load. I remember one night coming home from a particularly difficult board meeting. I felt beat up and ready to quit. It seemed like it was one issue, one failure, one criticism after another. Barbara met me at the door, and she knew something was wrong. She sat for almost two hours listening to me as I talked through the issues and unloaded my feelings. She held me and prayed for me. In the end I felt better and drifted off to sleep. But not Barbara. She lay awake long into the night processing all the emotions and thoughts I had dumped on her. Many a pastor's wife has lain awake long into the night wrestling with what her husband carries and praying that he would have the strength and wisdom to carry on.

Then comes the criticism aimed directly at her. "Our last pastor's wife was so caring … or such a good teacher … or raised six wonderful children who all went into ministry." Pastors' wives often feel totally inadequate for their role. Like their husbands, they give sacrificially only to hear about their weaknesses or failings.

While their husbands have a written job description as a starting point, pastors' wives face something abstract and unspoken. Every member of the church has a picture of what she should be like. Criticism comes from so many angles.

What criticisms have been leveled at your pastor's wife? Are they reasonable? Perhaps you need to examine your own actions and words toward your pastor's wife. It has been said that it takes one hundred positive statements to overcome one negative one. Criticisms stick. Look beyond the shortcomings and see the woman God loves!

Hardest of all for the pastor's wife are the criticisms against her children. In the next chapter we will talk about what it is like to grow up in a pastor's home. But for now let me simply say this: pastors' kids are like all kids—they mess up sometimes. All parents can get embarrassed when their children are caught doing stupid things. They also can get angry when their children are unfairly criticized. That's true for pastors and pastors' wives. But it is the wives who often take those criticisms the hardest. They carry the words and wounds inflicted on their children in the core of their being.

Criticism can be fair and constructive. But far too often the criticisms that come at pastors' wives are neither. Like exploding land mines, unfair criticisms can embed shrapnel deep in the heart of a pastor's wife and can eventually lead to bitterness and deep insecurities.

Understanding the pain of criticism, what actions can you take to protect and defend your pastor's wife?

1. **Look for the positives you see in your pastor's wife—and express them.** A genuine compliment makes the heart glad and gives encouragement for the role they have in the church.

2. **Become an advocate and a protector of your pastor's wife.** When unfair criticism is launched, don't be one of the silent majority. Stand for your pastor's wife and children. Let your pastor's wife be who God created her to be.

Minefield #3: Loneliness

Imagine being a part of a large community of people but never knowing whom you can trust and what you can say. Such is often the world of your pastor's wife. Too many have been wounded or betrayed in past experiences, so every word and every action carries a fear of what the consequences might be. The result is a life of loneliness.

The glass house in which a pastor's wife lives and raises a family creates its own loneliness. Not only is everyone watching, but the glass walls themselves separate the pastor's family from the people around them. A wife feels that separation deeply. Arriving at a new church where relationships are already established, they feel like the odd person out, trying to find a way into the circle. Expectations and criticisms make it even more difficult. Most do not feel the freedom to be who they really are, so they try to be who everyone wants them to be. Loneliness grows, and resentment builds. And just when they are beginning to find a rhythm and a place, their husband is called to a new church and it starts all over again.

Obviously, there are pastors' wives who find friends and security in the church they serve. But for most that is not the case.

They feel used and even abused by the church. They feel incredibly inadequate—often like a total failure. They feel like no one understands and that perhaps no one can. While their husbands gather occasionally with other pastors at conferences, rarely do they have the chance to talk with other pastors' wives. They feel isolated and alone.

One person alone cannot change this complex and difficult culture. But you can understand it and you can do something to minimize the loneliness. Your voice, your words, your actions can begin to move your church toward acceptance, empathy, and eventually appreciation for the person who bears the most difficult role in the congregation.

If you desire to extend a hand of friendship to the wife of your pastor, be patient if it is met with hesitation and apprehension. And above all else, don't offer and then fail to follow through, or betray the confidence. Better never to have reached out than to inflict another disappointment or wound.

Here again, pastors can unintentionally add to the loneliness of their wives. Early in my ministry I would go to important conferences with incredible speakers. I would come home energized and renewed. Barbara would have spent the week caring for four young children, two of whom were sick and two others who had fought all week. She got little sleep and felt like all she had done was clean up toys and change diapers. It was little wonder that she was not very interested in all I had to share when I came home. She was exhausted and at the end of her rope.

Whenever possible, send your pastor's wife along to those conferences. Let her spend time with her husband and with other pastors' wives. Find ways to provide childcare. These expressions of understanding and caring will bear much fruit.

At SonScape Retreats, we feel strongly about the need for pastors and their spouses to reconnect emotionally, spiritually, and physically. We have watched God restore relationships during our retreats because there is time for the couple to be together.

So in summary you can do more than you think to ease the loneliness of your pastor's wife.

1. **You can understand the complex world of a pastor's wife and why loneliness is so common.** Again, reading this chapter is a step in that direction. Instead of making assumptions, ask questions.

2. **You can offer friendship, understanding why hesitation and apprehension might be the response.** Let friendship happen; don't force it. Allow your pastor's wife to choose her friends. If you reach out, don't fail to follow through.

3. **Make it possible for your pastor's wife to accompany her husband to conferences and events.** Understand the importance of their sharing these times together. Provide the finances and, if necessary, childcare.

Encourage and Support the Marriage of Your Pastor and His Wife

One of the saddest things we face in working with pastoral couples is when ministry causes a pastor and his wife to drift apart. Bitterness replaces partnership. Anger replaces love. Finally, one or both partners become apathetic and are simply resigned to the fact that what is will always be.

Your church's concern for your pastor's marriage is an important part of keeping him healthy. Remember, many pastors' wives see the church as the other woman in their marriage. The pastor often gives his best time and energy to the needs of his congregation, leaving only scraps for his wife and family. Or at least that can become the perception.

PastorServe offers PastorCare, a great program for routine pastoral care. Among the components of the program is an annual marriage checkup. Every marriage could use something like that, but it is crucial for the pastor's marriage.

Marriage retreats, counseling, shared time attending conferences or seminars, or just a quiet couple of days alone at a cabin—these are crucial for your pastor and his wife. When your church or individuals in your church make these a priority, it speaks volumes to your pastor, but it speaks even more to your pastor's wife.

Again, no outside person can make the pastor's marriage healthy. That is the couple's responsibility. But you can let your pastor and his wife know that you recognize the importance of a healthy marriage for those called to lead your church. You can make times and tools available for them. You can send a note telling them you are praying for them and perhaps even enclose a gift card for an evening out together—on you.

Your pastor's marriage is critically important to you and your church because it is critical to *his* health and well-being. Invest in your pastor's marriage so that he can invest in yours as a pastor well equipped to lead and serve.

The Pastor's Wife Who Loves Her Role

Some women thrive in their role as pastor's wife. While I think the minefield of expectations, criticism, and loneliness is a danger for every pastor's wife, individual stories vary greatly. Sometimes it has to do with the church served, or the personality of the pastor's wife, or just the fortunate way things come together. Pastors' wives do not all experience lives of struggle and pain.

Barbara loved her time as a pastor's wife in a local church. Perhaps it is because we served a church plant and she was the first pastor's wife with no standard to follow. But Barbara would say it was also because she was given freedom to be herself. In the first year of our church plant, Barbara came to me and asked, "So what is my role as a pastor's wife?" I don't remember my exact response, but apparently I gave her an answer that made a huge difference. I said something to the effect of "Don't think of yourself as a pastor's wife. Just be who you are."

Barbara served in a variety of ministries and at one point took a year off from organized ministry during our twelve years at Maple Grove Covenant Church. She was at my side as much as possible with four young children. But all in all Barbara loved her role and people loved her.

There are many pastors' wives like Barbara: those who have avoided painful experiences or have been able to work through them. If your pastor's wife is such a person, appreciate what you have and encourage her all the more. It does not mean that the minefield does not exist or is any less dangerous for her. Your understanding, encouragement, and protection are still important. And above all else, surround her with your prayers.

The Pastor's Husband

Female pastors have been a part of some denominations for decades, but they are still a significant minority in most churches if they are there at all. As a result, there are some advantages and disadvantages to the role of pastor's husband.

On the advantage side, most churches have not figured out what to expect of a pastor's husband, so they leave him alone or just treat him as any other man in the church. Of all the pastors' husbands we have worked with (and we have worked with quite a few), I cannot remember one who struggled with congregational expectations.

The pastor's husband generally has his own career apart from the church. He may be asked to assume a duty or take on a responsibility at the church, but he is seen as a person in the congregation rather than as a pastor's husband. Clearly his role and the expectations that come his way look nothing like those placed on a pastor's wife.

Rarely is the pastor's husband criticized for not living up to people's expectations, because they have not figured out what to expect. Often they just leave a pastor's husband alone, which can lead to one of the disadvantages of his role. People can be awkward around him because he doesn't fit the norm. Most churches have years of developing the role of a pastor's wife, but what do they do when the pastor's spouse is a man? Should he be expected to play the piano? Should he serve in the kitchen? What exactly does a pastor's husband do?

Some men are very comfortable with themselves and almost enjoy watching people struggle with a situation outside the norm.

They engage with the church when and where they choose. Other husbands share the awkward feelings and stay in the shadows.

Pastors' husbands can struggle with learning how to let their wives lead. Many of them are leaders in their own worlds and have a difficult time keeping their thoughts and ideas to themselves—or at least waiting until they are asked.

Depending on the denomination, learning how to deal with the criticism of those who believe a pastor should not be a woman can be trying for a pastor's husband, to say the least. For some people it is an issue of biblical interpretation. For others it is a matter of preference. Either way they are talking about his wife's calling.

There are things that have been addressed regarding pastors' wives that can apply to some pastors' husbands. Perhaps one area that may be more difficult for the husband is to watch his wife be criticized, especially unfairly, and remain silent. Most men want to step forward and protect their wives. Figuring out when to let his wife fight her own battles and when to step in can be very hard on the pastor's husband.

Attending pastoral gatherings when spouses are invited can be especially challenging for a pastor's husband. Since the predominance of pastors in attendance are men, does he gather with the spouses or with the pastors? Does he go or does he stay away? Many simply avoid the gatherings. Obviously some denominations have more female pastors than male, which makes this less of an issue.

So how do you help when you have a pastor's husband in your church?

1. **Understand that everyone may be a little uncomfortable at first.** This is new for many churches and many people. Acknowledge the situation. Good things can result when our norms are shaken.

2. **Treat your pastor's husband as any other man.** He is a person more than a role. Honor him for his gifts and interests. Let him be comfortable as himself.

Whether wife or husband, the church body has a responsibility to support and care for the spouse of their pastor. What support and care look like depends on the individual person and the specific situation. But your investment in your pastor's life mate is an investment in your pastor's health and in the well-being of your church.

Take the story of Beth and Roger, for example. If only the woman with whom Beth had shared her heart had listened and prayed in confidence. If only the elders had encouraged marriage counseling and perhaps even made a financial investment in it. If only people had come alongside Roger and Beth in those difficult days of life and ministry. I wonder what impact such understanding and encouragement might have had on their pastor, his wife, their children, and the church itself. They might have all grown together into a church that could offer grace, truth, and love to a world of hurting people.

Think of what the impact might be if you and the people of your church would stand *with* your pastor and spouse. What if your church was not a minefield, but a safe place for pastor, pastor's spouse, and every person who walked through the doors? You can help make that happen.

Chapter 8

The Pastor's Family
Kids as Collateral Damage

Nothing is as painful for parents as watching their children struggle.

Jesus told the story of the prodigal son and his loving father. It is a story lived out in our midst all too frequently. And like the father in the story, many pastors ache as they watch their children walk away from the church and even from God. It doesn't have to happen. One person can make the difference. Maybe that person is you.

Pastors' kids (PKs) are exiting the church in huge numbers. It is a tragic subcategory in what is happening to pastors. PKs are the collateral damage. Amid all the things that can break a pastor's heart, watching his children walk away from the church is often the most devastating. I am a PK. My children are PKs. I understand the world of a pastor's kid from the inside and from the outside. It is a complex and difficult world.

"If this is what the church is like, I want nothing to do with it." Those are the words of many PKs who have been upended and blindsided by the conflict, criticism, and dysfunction they have observed and endured growing up in a pastor's home. They have seen and experienced too much, and it has left a negative impression on their tender young hearts.

Growing Up as a PK

Growing up in this world is not easy no matter how loving the parents and positive the environment. The father in the story of the prodigal son was generous, forgiving, patient, and above all, loving. His home offered every opportunity for his sons. Yet as good as the father was, neither son took the right road. Growing up as a pastor's kid can make the journey even more challenging.

A couple of chapters ago, we talked about how hard it is for a pastor to have one hundred bosses. Now imagine growing up with one hundred parents, most of them having a strong opinion of what is appropriate behavior for a pastor's child. The thought of having one hundred parents should alone give a perspective into the life of a PK. Everyone is watching *you*. So many people looking for so much from one so young. It is a heavy load, sometimes an impossible load to carry. Too many PKs are the deeply damaged, innocent bystanders in the tragedy of unhealthy pastors and/or unhealthy churches.

Some PKs thrive in their role. They are polite, behaved, and well mannered. They do their Sunday school lesson every Sunday. They are every parent's dream for a child. The church embraces them, and they embrace the church.

Many other PKs do not feel that embrace, and they are not sure they want it. They can be difficult, behave poorly, and resent the standards that are placed on them. They run in the halls, get into fights with the elders' kids, and never have their Sunday school lesson done. They feel like they will never measure up to the expectations placed on them. In time they simply quit trying.

Most people in a church expect PKs to look and act like the first group. They don't know what to do with PKs who fit more readily into the second group. Even the pastor and his spouse can be frustrated or embarrassed when their children's behavior is outside acceptable norms. They too can send hurtful messages, verbal and nonverbal, to their children, whom they love deeply. After all, PKs, especially their own, are to do and say the right things! Everyone knows that!

The writers of the Gospels tell the story of the disciples preventing children from approaching Jesus. Jesus rebuked them harshly, "Let the little children come to me and do not hinder them, for to such belongs the kingdom of heaven" (Matthew 19:14).

In every painting I have seen depicting that event, all the children appear so nice, clean, and compliant. I often wonder if among the actual children there were some who were strong willed, disobedient, and even defiant. I think there were. After all, the adults Jesus called were far from perfect, so why would we expect the children to be different?

Jesus did not say let the "good" children come to Me. He said, "Let the little children come to me and do not hinder them …"—all the children. Those who fit the norms and those who don't. I believe He took all of them in His arms and blessed them. The church needs to do the same. Too many PKs grow up resenting the role, the church, and even their parents. Some may have a faith in Jesus but they want nothing to do with the church. And I mean nothing!

Their rejection of the church is about not only the expectations placed on them but also what they experienced and observed in how the church treated its pastor. Many PKs have watched their father and mother sacrifice much, often too much, only to be mistreated or fired by the people they served so selflessly. The seeds of resentment are often planted in the growing child.

Barbara and I do not work directly with pastors' kids. But we have wept with far too many pastoral couples as they tell the story of their children who have become disillusioned, distant, and even bitter because of what they have seen in their home and in their church.

Those pastoral couples had no idea the toll that ministry would take on their families. If they had known, they might have thought twice before answering God's call to serve the church. The damage inflicted on their families is one of the most difficult and painful realities pastoral couples face. They ache so for their children.

Children are collateral damage in political and ethnic struggles all over the world. *It should never be so in the church.* All children, including PKs, should be safe there. But often they are not. Ask PKs and they will tell you stories of the wounds and losses they carry from growing up in a pastor's home and in the church their parents served. When conflict breaks out in a church, no matter what the issue and no matter who is right or wrong, many of the victims are children, often the pastor's kids. They often don't know what is happening, nor why, but they feel the insecurity and pain that result. It is time for the church to realize children are very much at risk in the tragedy that is taking place between pastors and people. PKs are often among the most vulnerable of those children.

The PKs in your church do not have to be collateral damage; but it will take action on the part of the people who attend your church, including you, to make that happen. Think about the PKs in your fellowship. Ask yourself what they are thinking and feeling. What scars do they already carry? Are you going to allow these precious ones to walk away from Jesus because of what was inflicted on them growing up in your church?

Consider these three essentials.

1. Treat Each PK as a Unique Individual

Every parent with multiple children knows how unique each child is. They can come from the same parents, be raised in the same home, be subject to the same rules, attend the same church, and yet be as different as night and day.

Barbara and I have four children. Three girls and a boy. Two are free spirits, and two like their world to be structured and organized. Three are somewhat compliant, and one is strong willed. One calls all the others on family birthdays and anniversaries to make sure they don't forget. Two border on obsessive compulsive. Three are very artistic; one is less so. And they all came from the same two parents.

Many people in the church expect all pastors' kids to be sweet, quiet, polite, and behaved. A large percentage of PKs do not fit that box. PKs, like all children, have different interests, talents, and personalities.

In addition—and you'd think this would go without saying— pastors' kids are *kids*, not adults. Like all kids, they are going through the stages of development. One of the most helpful insights Barbara and I learned had to do with equilibrium and disequilibrium. As children develop, they move from one level of equilibrium to another level of equilibrium. These are the good stages in which attitudes and behaviors are more in balance. But in order to move from one equilibrium stage to another, the child goes through disequilibrium. These are the periods in which life and behavior are in upheaval. The length of each stage varies greatly based on child and circumstance.

We have all wondered at one time or another about our own children: "Everything was going so well. What happened?" All children have difficult stages in their development. With our four children, it seemed like there was always one child, at least, in disequilibrium. Every Sunday someone was out of whack—whining, crying, complaining, or fighting.

Then there are the compliant children versus the strong-willed children. Compliant are generally easier than strong willed. Lucas was our strong-willed child. He was often taking risks or getting into trouble. There was a woman in our neighborhood who watched Lucas grow up, and years later when his name came up in a conversation, her comment was, "Is that kid still alive?" You get the picture.

Compliant PKs are more acceptable than the strong-willed ones. I remember two men who impacted my strong-willed son in his early years—one negatively, one positively. The first man took it on himself to correct what he saw as our parenting flaws with Lucas. Many Sunday mornings or Wednesday evenings he would come to tell me how he had caught Lucas misbehaving and had disciplined him.

I believe that children who are out of line need to be made aware of unacceptable behavior, but this man went beyond that. He was taking on the role of parent, because in his opinion we were not doing an adequate job. Over time his intervention began to negatively affect Lucas's attitude. Finally, I had to step in, not as pastor, but as Lucas's father, and tell the man to let me handle the discipline of my son.

Put that in contrast to the Sunday school teacher who sat under a table with Lucas on a particularly difficult morning, comforting his hurt feelings and loneliness. The man sat with Lucas the entire hour. He showed love to Lucas at a critical time, and it made a long-term impact.

Strong-willed children can be difficult. Every parent who has raised such a child knows how crucial it is to discipline without breaking the spirit. Strong-willed PKs need to know they are loved, not simply that their behavior is often out of line.

Children are very perceptive. They pick up on small things. If too many people send messages of disapproval to a young PK, the child begins to believe it. Just because a PK does not fit everyone's expectations does not mean there is something wrong with him or her. Instead, maybe there is something wrong with the expectations. PKs have all different personalities, interests, attitudes, and passions. They need to be accepted, loved, disciplined, and valued as the unique individuals they are.

2. Value What Is on the Inside More Than What Is on the Outside

A young pastor who was also a PK attended one of our retreats. Each day he wore a long-sleeved shirt, which was a little unusual for the weather. One morning I realized he had a tattoo under his sleeve. I asked him about it and its meaning. There was relief on his face as he rolled up his sleeve and showed me his arm.

Clearly he was afraid of my reaction if I saw the tattoos. As he shared his story, there was reason for his concern. Many times Christians had judged and diminished him for the tattoos that covered his arm as well as his upper body. Whatever your belief regarding tattoos and the teaching of Scripture, this young man was more than what covered his body. Long ago I learned that what is on the inside far outweighs what is on the outside. *Man looks on the outside, but God looks on the heart.*

If this is true for God, should it not be true for God's people? Certainly actions do make a difference, but it is the heart that matters most. Understanding a person's heart takes far more time and energy than simply judging behavior.

My children, Carissa, Meagan, Lucas, and Hillary, have all made errors in judgment along life's journey, but I know their hearts and am proud of who they are. Pastors' kids (like all kids) go through periods of bad attitudes and even poor choices. They are sinners like all of us. Unfortunately, too often they are held to a different standard than other children, a standard that is much higher, more rigid, and often grossly unfair.

Even if those standards are never spoken, they can be felt. I knew when people disapproved of my choices or behavior growing up, whether they said so or not. I saw it in their eyes. Sometimes I did not know what I had done, only that I had done something wrong. But there were also times when it was not just a look in their eyes; it was vividly displayed disapproval.

I grew up in the turbulent years of the '60s and early '70s. Music and dress were huge issues in the church at that time. One Sunday evening I came to church dressed in brushed blue denim bell-bottom pants with glistening turquoise vinyl pockets. My shirt was open three buttons down. (Don't ask me why—it was the era.) I was met by a church elder and told my dress was inappropriate and I should go home. Honestly, in those crazy days, I was just trying to find myself and understand life. There was no desire to be disrespectful to the church or to God. I was just trying to "be cool." But I still carry emotions of embarrassment and denigration from that evening.

But I also remember the church members who took the time to look long enough and hard enough to find my heart. I felt safe and supported by them along the ups and downs of my life. Their loving guidance had a profound impact on me.

Our oldest daughter was pretty compliant growing up. Overall she lived up to the expectations of those around her. After graduating from high school, she moved onto a college campus in the Minneapolis area. One night I received a phone call from her.

"Dad, I want to have my tongue pierced."

"You what?"

"I want to get my tongue pierced. I have thought about it for a long time and I really want to do this. I know you won't understand and you won't want me to do it. That is not why I am calling. I just want to be sure that if I do this, it will not change our relationship."

Her last statement caused me to stop in the middle of my shock and anger.

"Carissa, I cannot give you my blessing, and I don't understand. But this will not change my love for you nor my relationship with you."

When the call began, my eyes were on her action. Her question caused me to look at her heart instead. In the scheme of things, her tongue piercing lasted only a few months and was no big deal. But I could have focused on her choice and damaged our relationship for years to come.

If you are a parent, you know your children do crazy things and mess up at times. All children do. Some make poorer choices than others. When it comes to children, including the children of your pastor, look more at their hearts than their actions. Too many times our response to a poor choice or a wrong attitude sends a message that reaches beyond the action and into the core of the child. Sometimes it has a detrimental impact that lasts a lifetime.

Too many PKs feel like they are failures rather than that they simply failed. There is a big difference. "Failed" is about an action. "Failure" is about one's identity. The continual inability to live up to what people want or expect can crush a PK's self-esteem. "I can't be good enough, so why try?"

You can help the PKs who grow up in your church by looking beyond their actions and attitudes and into their hearts. Major on the things you see within them and minor on specific behaviors. When discipline is necessary, use the same standard you use with all children. Don't single them out because they are PKs. Above all, love them as you would any child.

With PKs, as well as with other children, look beyond what is and see what can be. Don't be among those who focus on the outside. Look at the heart.

3. Remember the PK's Story Is Not Complete

There are times when a PK's behavior goes beyond personality or poor choices in growing up. Sometimes there is defiant sin that not only is wrong but also is devastating to all involved.

A couple came to one of our retreats, brokenhearted. Their daughter had rebelled against everything they believed and valued, and a long series of poor choices led to the night she was out drinking with her friends. She decided to drive home but was in no condition to do so. There was a horrible accident and the woman in the other car was killed. Their daughter was sentenced to several years in prison for vehicular manslaughter. Can you imagine their pain?

Their story may be extreme, but there are so many pastoral couples whose children have become prodigals or who at least have made life-damaging decisions. There are PKs who are drug addicts, unwed mothers, agnostics, and alcoholics. Their parents ache to the core of their being. They spend many nights weeping and wondering where they went wrong as parents.

The last things they need are the judgmental attitudes from people in their church. Much of the time, people in the church are deeply sympathetic and compassionate in these circumstances. But it takes only one or two harsh, hurtful people to rip open hearts that are already bleeding, especially when the majority of people remain silent. Take a clear stand between these people and your pastor. Speak up and protect your pastor's family, especially in times of crisis.

But above all else in those times of devastating pain, the pastor and his wife, along with their child, need to cling to the truth that the story is not over. Our God is about redemption and restoration. Never give up on a prodigal PK—or any prodigal! Look at Scripture: Jacob was a liar and a cheat, David was an adulterer and a murderer, Paul persecuted Christians—but that was not their

whole story. One choice, one season of life does not have to determine who a person will become. If you can do nothing else, drop
to your knees and pray. Don't judge your pastoral couple, and
certainly not during the days they struggle with a prodigal child.
Instead, lavish your love and support on them.

Read your Bible and you will find many heroes of our faith
who had wayward and disobedient children.

Pastors are not perfect. Their parenting is not perfect. Their
children are not perfect. Bad things happen. Poor choices are
made. Heart-wrenching pain is experienced. Let your pastor and
their family be real.

Why does one pastor have four children that all seem to do
so well and even go on into full-time ministry, while another's
children all struggle and take the road of a prodigal?

I do not have an answer. I know so many parents who search
for an answer while their hearts are breaking over their wayward
children. I do know this—God is the ultimate Abba Father
and yet every one of His children went astray with only one
exception.

If you want to make a difference for your pastoral family in
times of pain and need, let them know you care, you're praying, and you stand willing to help if needed. Let them know you
believe their child's story is not over. Tell them you believe God is
still at work, still pursuing and redeeming their child.

How many times does God turn periods of sin and rebellion
into avenues of ministry later in a person's life? Don't view one
episode in a PK's life as the conclusion. Their story goes on! As
does yours.

How Can a Church or an Individual Influence a PK?

Remember the story of my being sent home for wearing trendy teen clothes to an evening service? That was a negative event in my life. But there were other moments that had a much different impact.

Growing up, I enjoyed theater. During my high school days, I came up with the wild idea that along with the kids in my youth group we could put on an Easter play. There were no adults involved. It was the dream of a group of teenagers. The play focused on the centurion at the cross and his flashbacks into past encounters with those who knew Jesus.

We sewed the costumes—girls, and even some guys, running sewing machines for the first time. We built the stage with props on the sanctuary platform. Yes, that's right, the sanctuary platform. A spotlight was rented and set up in an attic adjacent to the sanctuary where we removed a vent between the rooms and pushed the spotlight through. Individual scenes were practiced, but we never got around to going through the play from beginning to end. There was no dress rehearsal!

The night of the performance, all did not go smoothly. Actors stumbled in the dark. The spotlight came on at the wrong times. Lines were forgotten. But we made it through, and all in all it went okay. The people who came, mostly parents and regular churchgoers, gave us a nice round of applause.

The real surprise came the next Sunday morning when all the elders stepped up on the platform and invited all of those who were a part of the play to join them. They had made and signed a large document that they read to the entire congregation—thanking us for our performance the week before. They made it sound like it was a Broadway hit. (Let me assure you, it was not.) The congregation rose and gave us a standing ovation.

I will not forget that moment. It was over forty-five years ago, but I believe it was the beginning of my call into ministry. The people of the church believed in a group of ragtag kids, allowing us to mess up the sanctuary and try something we were excited about. This PK was changed forever.

When I became a pastor and had PKs of my own, I cannot tell you how much it meant to me personally when people genuinely loved and encouraged my children. My kids carry some wounds from ministry, but overall they were blessed with many people who figured out how to love them both in word and action.

Barbara and I came across some information at a business-coaching website that we have used often with our own children and frequently pass along to other parents. It originates from Bill Gothard's Basic Life Principles material. Whether or not you agree with all of his teachings, this particular insight gave us new ways of viewing some of our children's traits.

Called "Discerning Positive Qualities through Negative Traits," it is a list of negative traits, which if developed correctly, will lead to positive character qualities.[1] For instance, a child who is conceited, cocky, or overbearing could have the positive quality of confidence. Recklessness or harshness could be an indicator of courage. Daydreaming or mischievous tendencies may indicate creativity. Outspokenness, bluntness, or even brutality could develop into honesty. Read on. It's something to think about.

Discerning Positive Qualities through Negative Traits

Every negative trait is a positive quality misused. A person who is careless with money is misusing the quality of generosity. A person who is critical and judgmental is misusing the quality of discernment. Here is a further list of misuses:

POSITIVE QUALITIES	POSITIVE QUALITIES MISUSED (NEGATIVE TRAITS)
Alertness	Jumpiness; quick criticism; presumptuous inquisitiveness
Amiability	Gullible; status seeking; socially preoccupied; spineless
Analytical	Pickiness; fussiness; pettiness; over-attention to detail
Aspiration	Selfish competition; vain ambition; scheming
Compassion	Gush sentimentalism; undiscerning empathy; taking up offenses
Confidence	Conceited; cocky; overbearing
Cooperativeness	Compromising; conniving; lacking initiative
Courage	Recklessness; brashness; brazenness
Courtesy	Self-consciousness; social stiffness; superficial flattery
Creativity	Mischievous; crafty; daydreaming; devious
Decisiveness	Inflexibility; ruthlessness; dominance
Diligence	Slavishness; one-track mindedness; selfishly industrious
Discernment	Snoopiness; judgmental; critical; fault finding
Discipline	Rigidness; harshness; overbearing; tyrannical
Discretion	Over-cautiousness; secretiveness; timidness; undue carefulness
Earnestness	Nervous meticulousness; over-conscientiousness; over-seriousness
Efficiency	Perfectionism; fussiness; rigidness; impatience
Enthusiasm	Fanatical; overbearing; overwrought; aggressive
Expressiveness	Wordy; glib; vociferous; melodramatic

Fair-Mindedness	Indecisive; indiscriminate; undiscerning
Flexibility	Wishy-washiness; indecisiveness; spinelessness
Forgiveness	Irresponsible leniency; permissiveness; irresponsibility; weakness
Frankness	Tactless; insensitive; undiplomatic; disrespectful
Frugality	Stingy; miserly; penny-pinching
Generosity	Extravagance; spend thriftiness; wastefulness; squandering
Gratefulness	Flattery; gushiness; extravagant generosity
Honesty	Outspokenness; bluntness; brutality; indiscretion
Hospitality	Ingratiating; social climbing; cliquish
Humility	Self-abasement; extreme self-criticism; lack of self-confidence
Loyalty	Possessiveness; idol worship; blind obedience; undue attachment
Neatness	Perfectionism; over-meticulousness; intolerance; stiffness
Objectivity	Insensitivity; cold calculation; unloving
Patience	Indifferent; permissive; disinterested
Persistence	Stubbornness; inflexibility; self-willed; headstrong
Persuasiveness	Smooth talking; high-pressure tactics; pushiness
Punctuality	Intolerance; impatience with tardiness
Purposefulness	Single-mindedness; intolerance; inflexibility
Respectfulness	Idol worship; debilitating subservience
Resoluteness	Hardheadedness; closed-mindedness; stubbornness
Resourcefulness	Over-independence; manipulating; scheming calculation
Sensitivity	Touchiness; easily offended; emotional
Sincerity	Gullibility; over-seriousness; impulsiveness

A church can have great impact for the good if they believe in the young people who are a part of their community. That includes the PKs in their midst. Kids are messy and loud, often doing crazy things without thinking. But they are also soft clay waiting for loving hands to mold them and loving people to believe in them.

You can have a personal impact on the PKs in your church. Individuals can play such a positive role in the lives of young PKs. I remember well those people who loved and encouraged me along my journey. They invested time and energy into a kid with lots of ideas and not much wisdom. And there were others who committed themselves to praying for me as well.

One of the greatest ways you can help your pastor is to love and believe in his children. If you are not involved with them directly, then make them a part of your prayer life. If they make a mess along their journey, apply grace and encouragement liberally. Make sure they see love and affirmation when they look into your eyes on a Sunday morning or at a church event. Do not let the PKs in your church become collateral damage. Protect them, love them, and believe in them!

Chapter 9

Conflict
It's Inevitable

My heart went out to Phil. He was bringing a great deal of new ideas into a large, established, traditional South Carolina church. Reality hit home in a big way his very first Sunday. Following the morning worship service, Robert, a member of the congregation, approached him.

"I have a note to give you." Phil was puzzled. He inquired if the note was from Robert or if he were delivering the note on behalf of another. "This note is from someone very important in the congregation, and you are definitely going to want to read it. And I can tell you right now you aren't going to like it."

Phil continued to probe. "Is the note signed?"

"No," Robert replied, "the note is not signed, but please trust me, you need to read this immediately."

After some internal debate, Phil accepted the note, unfolded it, and read the following. "We are the largest donors in the congregation; we give close to five hundred thousand dollars annually. We are speaking for many families in the congregation when we say that there are three things that need to change by next Sunday. One, out of respect for the Lord Jesus, you need to preach in a robe. Two, the volume of the music needs to be scaled back from the ungodly ten (today) to a more reverent four or five. Finally, we need to sing a minimum of three hymns in every worship service. If these three changes are not immediately made, we will be taking our money elsewhere." And, big props to Phil, the next Sunday he preached in the same attire he had worn his first Sunday: slacks, nice shirt, but no robe. They sang one hymn, not three, and the volume stayed consistent. And the uber-wealthy family, true to their word, never returned. They told Robert to tell Phil that they went to another church where they would not encounter conflict, obviously failing to acknowledge they were going to drag a boatload of conflict behind them wherever they would go.

There are so many things wrong with that story, it's hard to know where to begin. Let's begin by acknowledging that conflict in the church is inevitable. The question is not *if* you will get your nose bent out of shape but *how long* it will take before your nose is bent out of shape. Remember, where two or three are gathered, predictably, there will be conflict. In the New Testament, we see Paul and Barnabas in a conflict (Acts 15:36–39). Even Jesus's own disciples, James and John, ended up in conflict with the rest of the disciples (Mark 10:35–41).

Conflict and Antagonists

One of my favorite verses in the Bible is Nehemiah 3:6. Nehemiah is recording in his journal the various teams working on the wall of Jerusalem. I'll start in verse 4 to provide some context:

> And next to them Meremoth the son of Uriah, son
> of Hakkoz repaired. And next to them Meshullam

the son of Berechiah, son of Meshezabel repaired. And next to them Zadok the son of Baana repaired. And next to them the Tekoites repaired, but their nobles would not stoop to serve their Lord.

Joiada the son of Paseah and Meshullam the son of Besodeiah repaired the Gate of Yeshanah. They laid its beams and set its doors, its bolts, and its bars.

Is verse 6, the final two sentences, not the best? Read it again. Nehemiah makes a note in verse 5 that a group existed who had no interest in serving. The nobles of Tekoite wanted nothing to do with this little building project, so they simply refused to work. So what is so great about verse 6? It's powerful for what it *doesn't* say. It *doesn't* say that Nehemiah called a special meeting and appointed a committee to study why the nobles were not going to work. It *doesn't* say Nehemiah went to the nobles and begged them to work. It's almost as if there is an unspoken sentiment between verses 5 and 6 in which Nehemiah is saying, "I'm not going to waste my time on you. I've got forty-one teams working on the wall. Forty and a half seem to be quite excited. In fact, that's everyone except you. Now, while I have no doubt that you would like for me to waste the next couple of months listening to your complaints and adjusting the project to appease your frustrations, that's not going to happen. And you want to know why not? Because I refuse to allow you, the antagonists, to set the agenda."

I wish every pastor would follow Nehemiah's lead. *Don't allow the antagonists to set the agenda.* If you are an antagonist, stop it! (If you aren't sure, ask a respected church leader to provide an honest evaluation.) Nothing you give or do or buy earns you the right to be an antagonist. Allow me to repeat myself. No amount of money you give to your church and no amount of time you have invested in your church has earned you the right to be your pastor's adversary. If you believe that the excessive amount of money you give to your church has earned you the privilege to make demands of your pastor that no one else in the church can make, I am reminded of Peter's words to Simon the Magician, "May your money perish with you" (Acts 8:20 NIV).

Clearly, the rich family in Phil's congregation believed their wealth purchased the right to be antagonists. They were sorely mistaken.

The Pursuit of Peace in the Local Church

Biblical peace is not the absence of conflict. Rather, peace is the active faith in Jesus Christ in the midst of conflict. Biblical peace creates a Christ-centered righteousness that brings people together in love. Peace is impossible without a radical change in our human nature. The Hebrew word *shalom* carries the idea of much more than the absence of trouble. *Shalom* means wholeness and overall well-being. In the days of the Old Testament for someone to bless you with the *shalom of the Lord* meant that he was asking that the Lord would bless you with a complete, full life. God's peace is not the absence of a negative—it is a positive. And yet, so many mistakenly confuse a cease-fire for biblical peace.

A husband and wife are arguing while they head to church. As they near the church, one of them says, "Let's not talk about this anymore. Good heavens—we're on our way to church!" And so they enter the worship service, smiling, holding hands, greeting others, while their conflict still brews just below the surface. They take their seats and prepare to be inspired by a pastor who surely doesn't argue like this with his spouse!

Meanwhile, in a room just behind the sanctuary, the pastor and the elders are engaged in a heated conflict. Impassioned words are exchanged. The elders are directing the pastor to address the budget deficit in the morning message. The pastor reminds the elders that they are about to enter into a worship service, not a business meeting. The worship leader sticks his head into the meeting and announces that the service is moments away from beginning. The pastor walks out of the meeting, knowing that his heart is unprepared to lead a congregation in worship.

Conflict all too often engulfs the local church. Yet conflict itself is not really the core problem. Conflict is like the check-engine light on your car's dashboard that tells you to look under the hood to see what's causing the real problem.

Matthew wrote, "Blessed are the peacemakers, for they shall be called sons of God" (5:9). But peacemaking is always a risk. Any attempt to be a peacemaker carries with it the possibility of misunderstanding or even failure. To be sure, it would often seem so much easier to let things slide in times of conflict. So many conflicts in the church take place because we have little idea how to biblically deal with conflict. There are five things you can do to promote a spirit of peace in your church. Your pastor would love for you to commit to practice these peacemaking practices.

1. Love Collapses Relational Triangles

First, commit to collapsing relational triangles. Collapsing relational triangles is one of the most practical ways to love your pastor. I consider Jay Fowler, one of the regional executive directors on the PastorServe team, to be an expert in the area of teaching churches how to collapse relational triangles. The following wisdom is straight from Jay.

Many Christians believe that a good Christian never gets angry with anyone. So when they do encounter conflict, they tend to deal with it by denial. When the conflict continues, if they are unwilling to deal directly with the person with whom they are in conflict, they may be tempted to go tell another person about their bad feelings toward the person with whom they are in conflict. When they do this, they have formed a relational triangle, a common but immensely *unhelpful* way of dealing with conflict. This inevitably results in gossip, more hurt feelings, and division in the church.

Mike and Heidi have served together on the worship team at church for the past three years. Mike is the full-time worship pastor, and Heidi is a volunteer who participates in singing on the worship team approximately twenty times a year. One particular month, Mike fails to schedule Heidi to participate in worship. It was an honest mistake on Mike's part, but Heidi is deeply offended, believing that Mike is intentionally sending her a passive-aggressive message that she should quit serving on the worship team. Mike and Heidi are now in conflict. Jesus said if we have a conflict with another person, we are to go directly to that person and talk with them about it (Matthew 18:15). The goal is to keep the conflict between just the two people so they can work at reconciliation. In this case, if Heidi would go to Mike, she would learn that the conflict was merely an oversight on Mike's part, a mistake he would readily own and immediately correct. But instead of going to Mike, Heidi chooses to go to Steve, another volunteer member of the worship team to share her frustration with Mike. Heidi has now created a relational triangle. If this sounds familiar, it's because relational triangles are the norm in many churches (and families and businesses and schools and governments and so forth).

There are three basic kinds of relational triangles.

Tell a Secret

In this triangle, Heidi goes to Steve and tells him why she is angry with Mike. They discuss all the ways in which Mike has wronged Heidi. How could Mike be so insensitive! Doesn't he know how much leading worship means to Heidi? The triangle is solidified when Heidi tells Steve that he can never mention this conversation to Mike. Steve is expected to keep Heidi's secret. After unloading her secret, Heidi feels a lot better. So much better, that she may never have any desire to go to Mike and actually resolve the problem. The bad news is, Steve now harbors bad feelings toward Mike. It *was* cruel of Mike to exclude Heidi from the worship schedule. Perhaps Steve should quit the worship team in solidarity with Heidi. Steve is now caught holding a secret and is unable to resolve the negative feelings he is developing toward Mike. He can't approach Mike without disclosing a confidential conversation, thus jeopardizing his friendship with Heidi.

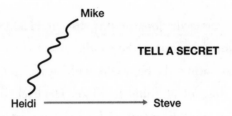

Send a Message

In this triangle, Heidi tells Steve to take a message to Mike. She tells him to let Mike know that she didn't appreciate being left off the worship schedule. "And tell Mike that I'm not surprised, because he has given hints over the past year that he doesn't want me around."

In families you might hear, "You tell your father how mad I am at him for not picking you up after school!" In a school it might sound like: "Tell that coach that my family and I did not appreciate the harsh language she used when correcting my daughter during the recent basketball game."

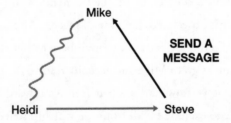

In this scenario, Heidi puts Steve in a terrible position. Try as he might, it is very difficult for Steve to get the message exactly right. When Steve delivers the message, Mike is caught off guard and begins to grill him about details. But Steve can't answer the questions because he doesn't know every detail of the conflict. He knows only what Heidi told him. Mike presses Steve, wanting to understand why Heidi feels this way and why she couldn't approach him herself. What does she mean when she says that she wasn't surprised because she saw this coming?

At this point, Steve is left with trying to make up answers or pleading ignorance. This can lead to an escalation of the conflict rather than a resolution. In the end, Steve feels like a failure and experiences the tension of being caught in the middle.

Send a Covert Message

The third kind of triangulation is similar to the second. This is when Heidi wants to send a message to Mike through Steve, but this time, Heidi wants to remain hidden and anonymous. Heidi wants Steve to approach Mike and say, "I just wanted to tell you that you really offended someone on the worship team. They asked me to tell you, but they did not want me to tell you their name. They just wanted you to know how hurtful and insensitive your actions have been."

Obviously, this kind of triangle causes many problems. First of all, it will make Mike feel paranoid. Since he doesn't know which specific person is upset with him, Mike will imagine that *everyone* on the worship team is upset with him! Once again, Steve feels caught in the middle, not wanting to divulge Heidi as the sender of the message, but possibly now feeling bad for Mike because he was able to hear that the offense was an honest oversight.

In a worst-case scenario, Steve can feel like he has a lot of power over Mike. Sadly, some people delight to be Steve in this scenario. They enjoy sending messages that hurt others, without having to take any personal responsibility, since, technically, the message belongs to someone else.

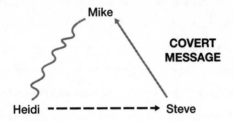

How to Collapse Triangles

The most important thing to remember is that there is a reason Jesus tells us to go to our brother or sister in private to work out our relational problems. It is because reconciliation can only happen face to face, between the two parties who are involved. When God had a problem with humanity, He showed up face to face in Jesus Christ to reconcile us to Himself. Since that is His way, He commands those who love and follow Him to do the same. As Paul says to the Corinthians:

> All this is from God, who through Christ reconciled us to himself and gave us the ministry of reconciliation; that is, in Christ God was reconciling the world to himself, not counting their trespasses against them, and entrusting to us the message of reconciliation. (2 Corinthians 5:18–19)

No one can apologize on behalf of another person. No one can confess sins that another person committed. Confession, apology, showing remorse, forgiving, and reconciling are personal acts that must be done between the two parties who have hurt each other.

How to Collapse the Triangle if You Are Steve

In this scenario, suppose you are Steve. When Heidi approaches you with a problem about Mike, Steve should say the following to Heidi:

1. "Have you had a chance to personally speak with Mike about this?" Steve might add, "I don't want to be in a triangle on this."
2. "Go talk with Mike as soon as possible. I will be praying for you."
3. "At the end of the week, I will check in with you to see if you had a chance to talk to Mike. If you did not, I will tell Mike that he needs to talk with you. I won't tell Mike what you said, only that there is an issue that needs to be resolved."

If Mike and Heidi cannot reconcile, Steve could offer to sit in with them or to find another mediator who could help them talk through their issues. This is in accordance with Matthew 18:16. If there is still a problem, Mike and Heidi could ask another pastor or one of the elders of the church to help in the reconciliation process. They might find it helpful to call in an outside resource, like PastorServe. This is in accordance with Matthew 18:17.

How to Collapse the Triangle if You Are Heidi

1. Speak directly to Mike. Go face to face to the person who hurt you. Avoid the temptation to triangulate. There may be times when Heidi needs to process her feelings with a trusted friend

like Steve. *But* that is only so she can go to Mike with a clear heart and head. Hopefully Steve will love Heidi enough to help her take the log out of her own eye. If Heidi does include Steve, it is important to report back to Steve how the meeting unfolded, so he gets to celebrate the reconciliation as well.

2. Go humbly. Be willing to admit to Mike your part in the conflict. As Jesus says, first take the log out of your own eye (Matthew 7:4–5).

3. Share honestly. The Bible exhorts us to speak truthfully (Ephesians 4:25). Jesus tells us we need to show our brother or sister their fault (Matthew 18:15). This should always be done respectfully and with grace (1 Peter 2:17).

4. Extend forgiveness. We have been forgiven so many sins by our Lord. We are right with God only by grace through faith in Jesus's death for us on the cross. He asks us to extend that same forgiveness to those who sin against us (Ephesians 4:32).

How to Collapse the Triangle if You Are Mike

Sometimes triangles are formed in churches because people can be dominant, prideful, unapproachable, and/or manipulative. People do not feel safe confronting this type of person. As a result, people may go to others and begin to triangulate out of frustration and fear. If you are Mike, here are some things you can do to help collapse triangles.

1. Be willing to go to a person who has something against you (Matthew 5:23–24).

2. Graciously receive people who come to you with a complaint or to work through conflict.

3. Find your security in Christ's grace for you. It is hard to hear criticism, but it is easier when we can freely acknowledge our own failings and sins and know that we are forgiven by our Shepherd.

4. Listen carefully to what is shared (James 1:19).

5. Repeat back what you hear the person saying to you. Sometimes that's all people need. They just want to know they were heard. They don't actually want you to change anything. They just want to be understood.

6. Find points of agreement in what they say. You may not agree with everything, but start with the places you do agree and focus on them.

7. Be willing to admit your fault, and ask for forgiveness (James 5:16).

8. Humble yourself, and be willing to learn (Proverbs 12:1). God may be trying to teach you something about yourself, your ministry, or your life.

9. Develop a preferred future together. In this case, how do Mike and Heidi want to go forward together? What can they agree to do in the future so they will not hurt each other? True repentance always leads to changes in how we live (Matthew 3:8).

God's heart is that we be at peace with each other (Romans 12:18). But He also knows that conflict is inevitable, even in His family, the church. So He asks us to do with each other what He modeled for us when He came in the person of Jesus Christ. No triangles. No secrets. No covert messages. He came to meet us, challenge us, and save us. He came so we could be forgiven and reconciled. And that is His heart for His family. That is what He wants us to do with each other.

2. The Passion Scale:
Die—Defend—Debate—Discuss—Dismiss

Second, do not unnecessarily escalate an issue. Many of the conflicts in the church are a result of accelerating issues to a place where they were never meant to go. In the local church, issues can fall into five different levels of concentration based on one's passion for that particular issue. Understanding these levels of passion and the appropriate response to each can dissipate a great deal of conflict plaguing the local church. The five levels are: die (centrality of faith), defend (core beliefs), debate (commitments), discuss (convictions), dismiss (choices).

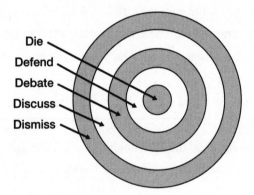

- Centrality of Faith — That for which we should be willing to **_Die_**

- Core Beliefs — That which we should be ready and able to **_Defend_**

- Commitments — That which we should be equipped to **_Debate_**

- Convictions — That which we should be willing to **_Discuss_**

- Choices — Personal preferences that we should be willing to **_Dismiss_**

First, there are issues for which we are intensely zealous. For these, we would be willing to give our lives. There are the hills that we are willing to die on. Perhaps you are willing to die for the doctrine of the Trinity or the fact that we are saved by grace and not by works. These issues constitute the *centrality of faith*. These are the issues for which we should be willing to *die*.

Second, there are issues that we should be passionately ready and able to *defend*. These are our *core beliefs*. Beliefs falling into this category commonly include church creeds, confessions, catechisms, and doctrine that is central to our particular church. For example, the Westminster Confession of Faith and the Heidelberg Catechism would commonly fall into this category.

Third, there are issues that we should be peacefully equipped to *debate*. These are our *commitments*. We have strong convictions in this level, though we readily acknowledge that there are mature believers who may hold a contrary position.

Fourth, there are issues that we should be willing to calmly *discuss*. These constitute our personal *convictions* and generally fall into areas of nondoctrinal personal preference.

Fifth, there are personal preferences that we should be willing to readily *dismiss*. These are *choices*. It would be nothing short of a waste of time to give this issue a minute of our time.

Commonly, the issues that divide churches are not the issues most would agree we should be willing to die for. The majority of conflicts in the church come from areas most would agree we should be willing to debate or discuss peacefully. Few church conflicts are centered on the atonement of Jesus Christ.

Severe conflicts arise in the church when we take an issue that most would determine to discuss or dismiss and we elevate it to an issue for which we would die. Examples abound. In the midst of a building campaign, the new carpet is chosen for the nursery, and suddenly people act like this is an issue for which they would be willing to die. The volume of music in the worship service suddenly becomes an issue for which a select group acts as if they would give their lives.

Or, even worse, an issue for which we should be willing to, at a minimum, defend is reduced to a personal choice. Look over the following list of issues. Where would you place the following: die, defend, debate, discuss, or dismiss?

Deity of Christ

Weekly Communion

Use of tongues in church

Style of worship

Specific Bible translation

Use of alcohol

Saved by grace through faith

Doctrine of the Trinity

Care for the poor

Drums in the church

Creation

Virgin birth

Baptism/sacraments

Church discipline

Expository versus thematic preaching

Biblical definition of marriage

Biblical inerrancy

Children in worship service

Eschatology

Sabbath rest

Church government

Role of women in the church

Personally, as I have matured in my faith (and in life), some of the issues I once passionately placed in the *defend* category (mode of baptism, role of women in the church, and form of church government, to name a few) have drifted into the *discuss* category, while some issues that were in the *debate* category (social justice, care for the poor) have moved into the *die* category. Presently, I have zero desire to debate you on the topic of infant baptism. Do I have strong views in this area? You bet I do! And yet, I have come to realize there are some highly intelligent Jesus followers on both sides of the issue.

How can you reduce conflict in your local church? Regularly evaluate if your level of passion for a particular issue matches where it falls on your passion scale. There may be some issues for which you need *more* passion. And there may be a number of issues about which you need to take a deep breath and realize that an issue you initially experienced a strong reaction to is actually a personal conviction, and nothing more.

Third, commit to be a peacemaker in your local congregation. Peacemaking characteristics include:

1. Active: Sometimes, peacemakers stir up trouble to bring about peace. They wage peace. Peacemakers actively pursue peace in all

of its fullness, encouraging well-being and wholeness. Jesus Christ is the Prince of Peace, and yet He created conflict (Luke 23:5). Paul the apostle—a champion of God's peace—caused riots nearly everywhere he traveled. And yet, it was Paul who wrote:

> Maintain the unity of the Spirit in the bond of peace. (Ephesians 4:3)

> So then let us pursue what makes for peace and for mutual upbuilding. (Romans 14:19)

> If possible, so far as it depends on you, live peaceably with all. (Romans 12:18)

2. Honest: Peacemakers admit failures in relationships, freely confessing that they are at odds with others (Jeremiah 6:14).

3. Willing to risk pain: It can be expensive to make peace. It can be humbling to make peace. Any attempt to be a peacemaker carries the possibility of misunderstanding and failure. Peacemakers frequently ask themselves if they are willing to risk pain and misunderstanding to make things right. They refuse to let sleeping dogs lie. Peacemakers are not content with status quo as long as there is no peace.

4. Commit to be protective of your pastor, remembering that peacemakers are committed to watching their pastors' backs. Commit to pray for your pastor. When in conflict, give your pastor the benefit of the doubt. If you hear a negative report about your pastor, do everything to collapse the triangle. Additionally, when

hearing a negative report about your pastor, remember there are always a minimum of two sides to every story. Remember this from Proverbs:

> If one gives an answer before he hears, it is his folly and shame. A man's spirit will endure sickness, but a crushed spirit who can bear? An intelligent heart acquires knowledge, and the ear of the wise seeks knowledge. A man's gift makes room for him and brings him before the great. The one who states his case first seems right, until the other comes and examines him. (Proverbs 18:13–17)

5. Never forget that there was nothing cheap about the peacemaking of Jesus, who gave His very life to accomplish ultimate peace (Colossians 1:19–20). Ephesians 2:13–17 reminds us:

> But now in Christ Jesus you who once were far off have been brought near by the blood of Christ. For he himself is our peace, who has made us both one and has broken down in his flesh the dividing wall of hostility by abolishing the law of commandments expressed in ordinances, that he might create in himself one new man in place of the two, so making peace, and might reconcile us both to God in one body through the cross, thereby killing the hostility. And he came and preached peace to you who were far off and peace to those who were near.

When the phone rings after 10:00 p.m., it's generally not good news. This particular call came at 10:35 p.m., and predictably, it wasn't good news. Brian, a sixty-year-old elder in a church where PastorServe had been consulting, informed me that he and his wife had decided to leave their church because they simply couldn't resolve a conflict with their new pastor. Brian explained that he had felt the God-given responsibility to confront Pastor Aaron regarding the unruly behavior of his young children. Apparently, Aaron's five-year-old daughter and seven-year-old son were running in the sanctuary following Sunday morning worship and Brian felt "the leading of the Holy Spirit" (his words) to make sure this behavior was immediately stopped. Following his "stern but loving" talk with the children, Brian told me that he was approached by Pastor Aaron who, in a sharp tone, told Brian that it was not okay for him to discipline his children. Brian went on to assure me that he had been a part of the church since before Pastor Aaron was born and no new pastor was going to correct him, particularly in the sanctuary to which he had sacrificially given to help build. Brian went on to tell me that since Aaron had arrived at the church, this was not their first confrontation. But "being the more godly man" (again, his words), Brian had forgiven Aaron and did not want to bring up past history as he had not wanted to reopen old wounds. He assured me that they had previously come to a place of peace, but this recent confrontation simply could not be ignored.

I probed into Brian's statement regarding reopening old wounds. I asked if he really believed the previous wound was healed or was just being ignored. If a previous wound has been ignored, the reopening of the wound can be the healthiest plan of action. Time does not heal all wounds. Furthermore, there is an enormous difference between biblical peace and a truce. What is commonly defined as peace in a local church is nothing more than a cold war truce in which conflict contributors have reluctantly agreed to a temporary cease-fire. Peace occurs when truth is known, brokenness acknowledged, issues are brought into the open, and parties reconcile. Peace never evades the issues. Peace never allows triangles. Although we all desire to avoid strife, if we sacrifice the truth, there is no real peace.

Once Brian had taken a deep breath, he admitted that while children running in the church was potentially a *debate* issue, his initial reaction had been more along the lines of *die*. Brian committed to pursue peace with Pastor Aaron.

Be a peacemaker in your congregation. Commit to breaking down triangles. Never allow a matter to become a *die* issue when it should be a *discuss* issue. Pray for your pastor that he would personally know the peace of God, which passes all understanding.

What's at Stake

I am a frequent flyer. Like many, my occupation involves travel. When I board a flight, the captain is often standing outside the cockpit door to greet the passengers as they board. We commonly have an exchange, which goes something like this.

> Me: Good morning.
>
> Captain: Good morning. How are you?
>
> Me: I'm doing good this morning, and how are you?
>
> Captain: Fine, thank you.

And with that, I smile, move down the aisle, and pray for an exit row seat.

Yet the conversation I really want to have with the captain goes something more like this.

> Me: Good morning.
>
> Captain: Good morning. How are you?
>
> Me: Me? Who cares how I'm doing! You're flying the plane! How are you? Did you get enough sleep last night? Everything okay at home? Are you feeling stressed? Did you have a big fight with your wife before you left for the airport

this morning? Is your teenage daughter creating
tension in the home? Did you shoot a 102 on the
golf course yesterday and you are just looking for
a place to vent your frustration?
Captain: Security!

I want a healthy, well-trained, experienced, stress-free pilot
flying the plane! Why? Because his bad day could become my bad
day. If he goes down, we are all going down.

Now imagine you board an airplane, put your bag into the
overhead compartment, and take your seat. The pilot comes on
the intercom and makes the following announcement:

Good morning, ladies and gentlemen. Welcome
aboard. Well, folks, there's a first time for
everything and today is my first flight. Now,
before you grab your bag and head for the exit,
let me assure you that first and foremost, I am
immensely qualified to fly this plane. I am a
math, physics, and computer science genius.
And I have undergone extensive flight training.
In fact, I graduated number one in my class
at FlyHigh University. I made A's in "Flying
Theory," "Landing Gear Deployment," "Peace in
the Cockpit," and "Flap Management." I took
every course in weather awareness, landing strip
design, and air traffic controller communication.
Now, to be honest, I have never actually flown

a plane, encountered real turbulence, or worked with a live team in the cockpit, but I did just fine on the simulator. So sit back and relax and enjoy the flight.

The fact is many pastors are not unlike this novice pilot. While the majority of Bible colleges and seminaries train pastors in theology, church history, and New Testament exegesis (all important areas of study), few teach classes in financial administration, conflict management, leadership development, and personnel supervision. Many pastors can read Greek but would have no idea how to read a spreadsheet, how to relate to a member of their congregation who is a CEO, or how to cast vision that will inspire the congregation. *Most pastors are untrained and ill equipped to face the challenges of pastoral ministry. The majority of pastors have not been trained for the challenges they face in pastoral ministry, which has led to an enormous gap between expectations and reality.*

Understandably, people want healthy pastors. They want pastors who are walking closely with the Lord, have a strong marriage, raise compliant children, pray regularly, serve the poor, and fast twice a week. They want pastors who do not struggle with everyday mundane sins. But this is an unreasonable expectation: "Whaddaya mean you struggle with lust? You're the pastor!"

Unreasonable expectations, coupled with enormous pressure to succeed, combined with an ignorance of the life and needs of a pastor, have led us directly into the center of a perilous pastoral crisis that is severely weakening the American church.

Crisis in the Church

There is a crisis facing the church today. It is a crisis of Christian leadership. It is not leadership skills that are at risk, but rather, the heart and soul of the pastor. For decades we have focused attention on developing ministry skills in our pastors while neglecting their inner life. Weary, wounded, depressed pastors reach deep inside week after week to find enough strength for one more sermon, one more crisis, one more counseling session. Then one day there is no more! As a result far too many pastors throw in the towel every month— they quit. Men and women with a passion and a calling who have nothing left to give.

Life is hard. Stress is a reality for most seeking to survive the brutal world in which we live. If you cannot measure up to the task, there is someone else who can. Should it not be the same with the men and women who serve our churches?

Let me say very clearly—your pastor's physical, emotional, and spiritual health should be a major concern for you. Healthy pastors are vital to the development of thriving churches, strong communities, and healthy families.

We live in an age of superstar pastors. Yet the reality is that the vast majority of pastors are not the definitive teacher, evangelist, missionary, and administrator rolled into one bundle of exegetical compassion. In fact, as discussed in the section on pastoral capacity, the expectations placed upon pastors border on the ridiculous. These unrealistic expectations have led pastors into a position of inexpressible fear. One pastor recently told me, "I have to hit a home run every week. When I come back to the bench—I immediately start thinking about my next at-bat—and that I need to hit another home run."

Odds are, I have never personally met your pastor. But I can guess that your pastor is an amazing human being. I have often been with pastors in the aftermath of natural disasters. I was with pastors shortly after Katrina devastated the Gulf Coast, after a tornado tore through Joplin, and after Haiti was rocked by an earthquake. One thing is clear: *Pastors are the first in line to give help and the last in line to receive help.* This mind-set has led a multitude of pastors to *not* receive the love, support, and encouragement they so desperately need.

This book was designed to help you, the church member, care for your pastor. Plain and simple, *your pastor needs you because pastors are people too.* Your pastor needs your support, encouragement, and prayer. Above all, your pastor needs you to understand that he is a real person. He struggles with sin—the same as you. Like you, he is tempted in the areas of pride, lust, greed, jealousy, envy, anger, and gluttony. And like you, he wants to keep his job, which results in an understandable cautiousness when expressing his deepest life issues.

Your pastor does not want you to think of him as the ultimate voice of God, who alone can speak truth in the most difficult of circumstances. *Your pastor needs you to understand that he is, in so many ways, just like you.* He needs God's grace just as much as you need God's grace. Few would argue that the local church is God's plan A to reach the world with the message of Jesus Christ. And, undeniably, God in His infinite wisdom has called broken people to serve as leaders within the local church. The leader of broken leaders is the pastor.

Here's the silver lining—congregations need to understand that pastors do want to love their people well. They want to lead well. They need support and encouragement from their congregation. They long for the church to create a secure environment for admission of incompetence in particular areas of ministry and acknowledgment of personal brokenness. This only comes about as the pastor believes and lives gospel grace before the congregation.

Pastoral ministry has been determined to be one of the most stressful jobs in America, ranking only behind college president and hospital administrator. The stress is the result of the unending, intense, continuous care responsibility of pastors. The role of a pastor can be likened to a medical doctor who sees terminal patients for hours on end every day. Because of this, the pastor must set personal limits for himself to maintain balance, develop relationships outside of the church, and be in a support group with other pastors.

The call to be a pastor is a call to the impossible. Your pastor is crucial to you, your family, and your church—but he will fail in his calling without your help.

This book is a field guide to help you care for your pastor. Your pastor needs you. He needs your encouragement, prayers, love, and affirmation. Your pastor needs you to grant him the freedom to take risks and fail. Your pastor needs you to give him the freedom to preach grace, live grace, and experience grace. It is our prayer that this book has assisted you as you seek to extend care to your pastor.

Acknowledgments

A huge thank-you to Dan Rich, Ingrid Beck, and the wonderful team at David C Cook for believing in this project. Apart from your vision to serve pastors, there would be no PastorServe Book Series. Thank you for loving pastors and the local church, in the USA and around the world.

Thank you to our editing team, particularly Jamie Chavez.

Thanks to Andrew Wolgemuth for being a great (and patient) friend and agent. We could not have walked this road apart from your guidance.

Above all, we are eternally grateful to the Lord Jesus, our Great God, Savior, Redeemer, and King. We pray this book glorifies Your name, advances Your kingdom agenda, and blesses the church and those whom You have called to lead in the role of pastor. *Soli Deo gloria.*

From Larry

I am grateful to Bob and Sandy Sewell, who founded SonScape Retreats as a safe place where those in ministry could come away for rest and renewal. In one of their earliest retreats, Barbara and I, as a young ministry couple, experienced their loving care and were introduced to the importance of spiritual retreat. It changed our lives and our ministry.

Now as the president of SonScape Retreats, it is my privilege to serve with an extraordinary group of people. Mike and Sandy Schafer, Greg and Connie Kennedy, Vicki Ceass, Perry and Jeanien Meyer, Thane Barnes, Rob and Shini Abraham. Your friendship means more than you know. Your commitment to pastors, missionaries, parachurch leaders, and their spouses has impacted thousands of lives across the years, including mine.

Thank you to the SonScape board of directors for their support of this project and specifically to authors Steve Rabey and Verdell Davis Krisher, who invested much time and energy in helping a novice writer communicate clearly.

To the people with whom I served at Maple Grove Covenant Church in Minnesota for thirteen years—you cared well for your pastor and his family. I was one of the fortunate ones who served a congregation that loved and supported their pastor. There are too many names to mention, but I count it a great privilege to have worked with such an amazing group of people. Lives were changed, God blessed, and together we learned what true Christian community is like.

To my dad, who taught me much about ministry, and my mom, who filled our family with laughter and joy—thank you! My brother and my sister, along with their families, have become treasured parts of my life and journey.

Finally, to my own family, who lived the life of a pastor with me. My beloved wife, Barbara, who is my life partner, ministry partner, best friend, and much more than I could ever have dreamed. Every day is an amazing adventure! To my four children, Carissa, Meagan, Lucas, and Hillary—PKs all—I love you dearly and am so very proud of each one of you. My heart is full of so many wonderful memories and to this day you bring me joy when the days get difficult.

From Jimmy

First and foremost, thank you to my wife, Sally, for her incredible love, support, and encouragement. I could not have asked for a better best friend, spouse, and partner in life and ministry.

Thank you to my family for their consistent love, encouragement, and support. To Mark, Holly, Ivy, Megan, Sarah, Paige, and Allie, I pray that each of you will find your deepest satisfaction in following Jesus all of your life. And I hope you will find less satisfaction destroying me in every board game imaginable.

A huge thank-you to my coauthor, Larry Magnuson. Writing with a dear friend who loves pastors as you do is an incredible privilege. I look forward to many more years of partnering together in ministry.

Thank you to the PastorServe team for the joy you bring me each day as I am allowed to serve shoulder to shoulder with you. In particular, thank you to Jay Fowler for your enormous help with the conflict chapter, Wesley Horne for insight into pastoral capacity, and Dan Dermyer for writing the prayers for pastors. Thank you to the PastorServe board, particularly Jim Dodd for your support in this project (yes, PastorServe has a board member with the same name!).

I am eternally grateful to my brother Kenny for introducing me to Jesus and the local church. Watching you consistently love Jesus and the church for forty years has brought me great joy. You are an incredible pastor.

Writing a book on how to care for your pastors reminds me how grateful I am for the pastors who have significantly impacted my life by pouring their lives into me as my pastor. Thank you to George Wood, Jerry Root, Kent Hughes, Howard Clark, Paul Borthwick, John Wood, and Bernard Franklin. Thanks to my home church, Redeemer Fellowship in Kansas City, especially Brian Key, Evan Rosell, and Rachelle Crowe. Thank you for lovingly pastoring my family.

Thank you to those who have gone to extraordinary lengths to love my family. As your pastor, you lightened my load and brought me great joy in the journey of pastoring God's people. You are models of what this book is all about. A special thank-you to Olena Mae Welsh (with Jesus), Bob and Cynthia Fantasia, Roger and Becky Sandberg, Rich and Karen Aiken, Paul and Janet Catalana, Scott and Kathy Gulledge, Mark and Kelli Williams, Mark and Jan Batten, Tim and Olivia Smith, Dan and Mary Wolgemuth, Jim and Deb Fenlason, Dave and Darla Blue, Jeff and Darraugh Gott, and John and Joy Edmundson.

A big thank-you to my dear friends and partners at Nehemiah 3, particularly Frank Brown, Doug Freeman, and Brad Clark. This journey has largely been made possible because of your generosity.

A heartfelt thank-you to Gary Ascanio, my most faithful prayer partner.

A Vision of a Healthy Church
A Case Study of Friendswood Community Church

In 1997 Rick and Marie Baldwin, along with four other couples, launched Friendswood Community Church in Friendswood, Texas. Their overriding passion was to introduce people to Jesus, helping them to become fully devoted followers. The primary vehicle for evangelism in those early years was a casual, contemporary worship service with practical, biblical, evangelistic preaching.

Friendswood Community Church (FCC) began in an elementary school that demanded many hours of setting up and taking down each Sunday. The commitment required on the part of the small leadership team was overwhelming at times. Rick and Marie, along with their small board of directors, invested themselves passionately into the launching of the new fellowship.

During the second and third years, God blessed the fledgling church with significant growth. Many came to Jesus. Small groups were started as a way to disciple the new Christians that were flooding to the church. But that meant the workload only increased for the core leadership. The five couples agreed to invest themselves completely in the new church in those early years, but they also recognized if they were to remain healthy for the long haul, better patterns would have to be developed. Together they committed to be a church where the health of the leadership was a vital core value.

While Friendswood Community Church experienced an exciting launch and significant growth in the early years, there were also major bumps along the way. Issues with staff members led to conflict and even departures. Groups within the congregation took sides and people left. Developing a community of people was messy, as it always is.

Growth, building programs, additional staff, new ministries—they all added both to the excitement and to the unhealthy pace. Action had to be taken. It was during that time that Rick and the board of directors began to develop a plan to keep Rick and Marie and other staff members healthy within the context of an exploding church.

Friendswood Community Church is not perfect. Mistakes have been made along the way. I offer them not as the ultimate example of a church caring for pastor and staff, but as one that is making a determined effort and with significant progress. It can only happen when pastor and church leadership, along with all who attend, truly make health a core value. It takes continual effort, and a willingness to fail followed by a determination to get up and get after it again. Friendswood Community Church is a good example of that commitment and determination.

Understanding the Pastor and the Church

Rick is a visionary and an introvert. He sees the big picture of what can be, but he also needs time alone in reflection and renewal.

Without clear boundaries Rick would soon burn out and burn up. In 2002 Rick and Marie came to a SonScape Retreat. Understanding who they were was a significant part of their time with us. They realized their need for clear boundaries as an essential part of their plan for long-term ministry health.

Rick is also highly organized and highly structured. While he cares deeply for people and has very good relational skills, continual interaction drains Rick. Sermon preparation and preaching are labors of love. Strategic visioning and organizational oversight are the things that are more energizing for Rick.

It is crucial for a pastor and a church to understand who they are—both strengths and weaknesses. Because FCC was a church plant, it did not wrestle with old, established patterns of operation and behavior. Most churches do not have that luxury. Every church and every pastor have personalities and behaviors. They have blind spots and weaknesses. Neglecting to understand who a church is and who the pastor is will result in unnecessary conflict and criticism. There are a variety of tools available to increase understanding of pastor and church. Self-discovery and self-understanding are essential if you want your church to be healthy. Rick and his leadership team were committed to deepening their understanding.

In 2008 Barbara and I were invited by Rick and the board of directors to do some work with them to increase their self-understanding and awareness. We used the Myers-Briggs Type Indicator. There was a significant "aha moment" when all realized Rick was the only visionary dreamer on the board. The rest of the board was made up of individuals who lived and focused on the right here, right now. Rick saw what could be and the members of the board focused on what was. The recognition clarified many misunderstandings among the team. What they learned helped them recalibrate their expectations and team structure. Healthy churches and healthy pastors are continually developing their understanding of each other in order to better lead their people.

Church personalities are often influenced by the personality of their pastor. Rick is an introverted visionary with strong organizational, administrative gifts. He likes things clearly structured and clearly communicated. Because FCC is a church he founded, it has taken on many of his strengths as well as some of his weaknesses. Between Rick, his staff, and the board, Friendswood prides itself on functioning as a well-oiled machine. That does not mean they are always successful, but that is their goal.

When a church is highly organized with clearly stated expectations, accountability structures, and reporting, people with those same giftings thrive in the environment. The ones who may struggle in such an environment tend to be the creative, free-spirit types. When a church or lead pastor is creative and free spirited, it is typically the organized-structured types who struggle. No church is good at everything.

By understanding the personality of the church and the lead pastor, the leadership can be aware of staff hires who should thrive in the environment and those who may struggle—even though they are essential to the church's mission.

All that to say, it is important to keep in mind who FCC and Rick Baldwin are as we explore what they have done to build a healthy environment for church and staff. Their approach may not be fully applicable to all churches and all pastors. But they are giving the issue of staff health and understanding significant attention, and their efforts are producing very positive results. Again, remember there is no plan that fits every church. The issue is not having it all together—the issue is whether it is a priority that is getting appropriate attention.

Clear Expectations

The leadership team of FCC recognized the importance of clear expectations for the key staff members. After much prayer and discussion they came up with the following.

EXPECTATIONS OF KEY STAFF

DEEPLY PURSUE FULL DEVOTION TO CHRIST

- Live out your faith with a radical obedience to God.
- Pray daily.
- Study the Bible daily.
- Participate in authentic worship by faithful attendance at Sunday morning services.
- Immerse yourself in the life of an FCC small group.
- Serve in your area of giftedness.
- Manage your finances biblically.
- Practice evangelism.
- Observe a weekly Sabbath that is restful, renewing, and God focused.

DEEPLY PURSUE FULL COMMITMENT TO PERSONAL DEVELOPMENT

1. Exhibit exemplary Christlike character.

- Have a teachable spirit.
- Ascribe to a strong work ethic by pouring your best effort into a forty-five-to-fifty-hour workweek.
- Be a role model to other staff members and volunteers in planning and performing your job.
- Show respect to others by being on time for all meetings and appointments, both professional and personal. When circumstances prevent this, communicate your delay with the appropriate parties.
- Follow through in a timely fashion on all commitments and promises.

2. Be a highly self-disciplined self-starter.

- Be proactive in your ministry role by taking the initiative to intentionally seek and implement new ideas to improve your area of ministry.
- Exhibit appropriate self-discipline to implement ideas with minimal supervision.

3. Proactively learn and grow in your area of expertise and ministry.

- Develop an annual plan for professional growth that includes clear goals for the coming year.

DEEPLY PURSUE COMMITMENT TO FCC

1. Be a consummate team player who seeks what is best for the church.

- Value the greater good of the church over the greater good of any ministry.
- Pray for other leaders of the church.
- Give verbal affirmation to other leaders of the church.

2. Be publicly supportive of all other staff, leadership, and ministry direction.

- Encourage and support all other ministries of the church by occasionally attending ministry events outside your own.
- Always speak positively of all of the efforts of ministries and leaders.

DEEPLY BELIEVE AND INVEST IN WHAT GOD IS DOING AT FCC

1. Give a minimum of a tithe to further God's work at FCC.
2. Foster a grace-filled environment.

- Lead with love.
- Use kindness in conveying both compliments and criticism.
- Practice Matthew 18:15 with the goal of reconciliation.
- Speak the truth in love.

Some people may be overwhelmed with such a detailed list of expectations, but it does give a clear baseline for understanding what is expected of every staff member and in turn what they can expect from other staff.

The list may be a little too specific for me as one of those visionary, free-spirited types, but I highly respect the work that Rick and the leadership team have done to communicate their expectations clearly. Many churches have not done the hard work of clarifying what their basic expectations are. Whatever the level of detail, such a list helps pastor, staff, church leadership, and church member to understand the primary expectations by which they will be evaluated.

In addition, FCC has individual job descriptions for each person's position, including who they are responsible to and how their efforts will be measured. Reviews and accountability are clearly communicated.

Reasonable Compensation

FCC lets its staff know that while they will not get rich in their positions, they will be taken care of adequately. The board works to compensate their staff above the national average for people in similar positions. It is in the arena of benefits that FCC has chosen to go above and beyond the norms.

- **Health insurance.** FCC pays the full premium for a health care plan for the staff member and family. "We want every staff member to have protection from a catastrophe that would otherwise threaten their security as a family."

- **Disability insurance.** FCC also provides disability insurance protecting its staff in an unforeseen crisis that would prevent them from continuing in their position and receiving their compensation.

- **Life insurance.** Each staff member has a life insurance policy to help provide for the family in the case of an unexpected death of a staff member.

- **Aggressive pension program.** FCC wants all staff members to have adequate retirement funds. "We don't want a former pastor standing out on the street corner or sleeping in a shelter." The board has set up a very aggressive pension program for its pastoral staff.

- **Days off, Sabbath, vacation, and sabbaticals.** "We value time away from the job as an essential part of a healthy work pattern." Rest, play, and time away—these are all encouraged at Friendswood Community Church. A week for spiritual renewal is given to each staff member over and above their vacation time.

While every church may not be able to do as much as FCC, every church can do something. Most churches can do more than what they are doing. Compensation and benefits are important elements in keeping pastors and staff healthy in ministry.

Help Made Available

FCC makes help available to pastoral staff through their direct supervisor and board relationships. While every staff member may have individual opinions on what is available and what more could be available, overall FCC is working hard to make needed help available to the staff. FCC has significant funds set aside each year for outside help for pastors. Opportunities include:

- **Mentoring and coaching.** Every pastor benefits from a coach and a mentor. Coaches and mentors are individuals with gifts and training in assisting pastors in more clearly developing their gifts and mission. FCC promotes these relationships and even helps with costs as is necessary and possible.

- **Counseling.** Personal or marriage counseling is available for pastors and for their spouses. "We believe that counseling for our staff is critical and that is it equally critical to make it available for every pastor's spouse."

- **Continuing education.** FCC wants its pastors to develop their vocational talents as well. Funds are set aside for specific continuing educational opportunities on a regular basis.

- **SonScape Retreats.** FCC sends multiple pastoral couples on their staff to a SonScape retreat each year. The week is an investment in their marriage and in their spiritual health. In addition FCC brings Barbara and me (Larry) to their church

every few years to meet with pastors and board
to continue an investment in their spiritual and
marital health.

FCC recognizes that investing in pastoral health on the front
end often prevents crisis on the rear end. They are making an intentional investment in pastoral health and well-being, wanting every
staff member to be healthy at the core. FCC is committed to being
proactive, leaning into issues before minor issues become major ones.
They believe every church would benefit from investing in an overall
plan for the health of their pastors.

"SonScape Retreats helped us build a foundation and framework
for a healthy staff and a healthy church," says Rick and the FCC
board of directors.

An aggressive plan working toward pastoral health benefits the
entire church. It takes time and energy to produce and refine, but it
will save the church countless hours wasted in conflict and misunderstanding. More than that, it is an investment in leadership that
bears much long-term fruit.

Appendix B

Praying for Your Pastor
Why Is It So Important?

As you have read in this book and know from your own experience, the work of a pastor is multifaceted, complex, and seemingly never finished. Pastors have some of the same concerns shared by most everyone; *plus* they face some of the most complicated tasks of any large corporation *and* they work within the nuanced realm of interpersonal relationships. To tackle this work requires wisdom, maturity, vision, gifts, and perseverance. God's work accomplished for God's glory requires God's servants to labor with the strength and guidance that *only* He can provide. Personally, every pastor needs to pray. And every pastor needs others to pray with him and for him. Prayer is vital to the work of God.

The apostle Paul concluded many of his letters with the request, "Pray for me." He knew that he needed God's leading and help if he were to do God's work. Every pastor today needs God's help too. It is all part of doing God's work God's way, for God's glory.

Pray for Your Pastor

In order to help you pray for your pastor, PastorServe offers several text- and app-based resources. You can enroll to receive a *daily* or *weekly* text reminder on your mobile device. Each prayer text will help to focus prayers for your pastor. Additionally, each prayer text is accompanied by a link to a scripture that offers additional direction in praying for your pastor.

These prayers have been written from two different points of view. First, some prayers are designed to help you pray for your pastor as a person, for spiritual growth and maturity as a follower of Jesus. Because your pastor is a person, anything you pray for yourself or anyone else can be prayed for your pastor. Second, there are specific aspects of your pastor's life and ministry that require prayers to be directed toward pastoral work. Some of the prayers offer a brief glimpse of tasks your pastor will face that are particular to pastoral ministry.

You can join in with others who are praying for their pastors by texting the word "pastor" to 74574 or by following the link on the PastorServe website, http://www.pastorserve.net/engage/pray/. Additionally, we encourage you to download the PastorServe App available for both Apple iPhone and Android devices. The app is specifically designed to help you love, pray for, and encourage your pastor.

If you aren't tech savvy (or even if you are), we encourage you to pray daily for your pastor using the following *Thirty-One Days of Prayer for Your Pastor*. These prayers focus on the personal and pastoral life of pastors addressed in this book and provide a foundation to begin regularly praying for your pastor.

Day 1

Pray for your pastor's work—to strengthen the weak, heal the sick, and bind up the injured (Ezekiel 34:4). Pray for your pastor's care and outreach, searching out the lost and bringing back the stray (verse 5). Pray for your pastor's diligence, to care for the flock more than they do themselves (verse 8).

Day 2

Pray for your pastor's reliance on God for help in caring for those who belong to God (Ezekiel 34:11). Pray for your pastor's tenderness—to provide the sheep good grazing land and still water (verse 14). Ask for justice in your pastor's ministry, that your pastor would not overlook any, but care for all (verse 16).

Day 3

Pray for your pastor's wonder, for jaw-dropping awe at God's love for sinful people (Romans 5:8). Pray for your pastor's hunger for God, that God's name and renown be the desire of his heart (Isaiah 26:8). Pray for your pastor's joy, for satisfaction by streams of living water flowing inside of him (John 7:37).

Day 4

Pray for you pastor's renewal, that God's grace would be sufficient and His Word would be fresh (Psalm 19:7). Pray for your pastor's contentment—for deliverance from coveting what belongs to others (Exodus 20:17). Pray for a repentant heart for your pastor and that God would make every sin a reminder of the cross (1 John 1:9).

Day 5

Pray for your pastor's holiness, for no self-satisfaction apart from Christ (Philippians 3:9). Ask also for your pastor's wholeness, for grace to be holy, kind, gentle, pure, and peaceable (James 3:17).

Pray for your pastor's honesty, to reject deceptive ways and state the truth plainly (2 Corinthians 4:2). Pray for your pastor's growth, that he would contemplate the Lord's glory to become more like Jesus (2 Corinthians 3:18).

Day 6

Pray for people to help your pastor, for men like Aaron and Hur who helped Moses pray (Exodus 17:12). Pray for friends for your pastor, for those who will listen, pray, and even confront them in love (Proverbs 17:17). Pray for a coach for your pastor, for one who will share personal experience in ministry (2 Timothy 4:11).

Day 7

Pray for coworkers for your pastor, to share in such an important and daunting task (Numbers 11). Pray for a mentor for your pastor, for one who will share his life as well as ministry (1 Thessalonians 2:8). Pray for a counselor for your pastor, for one who knows the heart and how to walk with God (Proverbs 11:14). Ask God to provide those who will encourage your pastor to continue in ministry and not give up (Galatians 6:9).

Day 8

Pray for your pastor's vision, to seek the welfare of the city, doing good for Jesus's sake (Jeremiah 29:7). Pray that your pastor recognizes common grace, that God sends rain on both the just and the unjust (Matthew 5:45). Pray that your pastor rejoices in special grace, that his heart is aligned with all in heaven who party when a sinner repents (Luke 15:10).

Day 9

Pray for your pastor's concern for the lost, for a burden regarding their status before God (Matthew 25:46). Pray for your pastor's zeal for the lost, that they pray and work for those who do not know Jesus (Romans 10:1). Pray for your pastor's evangelism, for confidence in holding out the word of life (Philippians 2:16). Pray that your pastor not be ashamed of the gospel, but speak it boldly, as he should (Ephesians 6:20).

Day 10

Pray for your pastor's daily walk with Jesus, to hear, know, love, and follow the Good Shepherd (John 10:4). Pray that in walking with Jesus, your pastor would bear much fruit, and for pruning by the Word to make him more fruitful (John 15:2). Ask that your pastor remain thankful always, seeing the Lord's hand in all things (Ephesians 5:20). Pray that your pastor would find great joy and comfort in Jesus and not in themselves (Galatians 2:16).

Day 11

Pray that your pastor keep first things first by focusing on prayer and ministering the Word (Acts 6:4). Pray that your pastor's prayers be genuine, not to be seen by men, but to be heard by God (Matthew 6:5). Pray that you pastor be diligent in prayer and not give up (Luke 18:1).

Day 12

Pray that out of His glorious riches, God would strengthen your pastor through His Holy Spirit (John 14:16–17). Ask that God would dwell in your pastor's heart through faith, and that your pastor would be rooted in the love of Christ and have power to know it more (Hosea 6:3). Pray that your pastor would not be alone but, with all the saints, would grasp the love of Christ and be filled with the fullness of God (Ephesians 3:16–19).

Day 13

Pray that your pastor's marriage be strong, vibrant, and reflect Christ's love for the church (Ephesians 5:25). Pray that your pastor and spouse would cultivate their marriage and cherish their partnership in life (Genesis 2:25). Pray for clear and open communication in your pastor's marriage (Ephesians 4:25–32).

Day 14

Pray that your pastor guard their time and energy so they can serve their family well (1 Corinthians 7:28). Pray that they seek God's protection and blessing (Job 1:5). Pray that your pastor's family would not feel cheated by ministry but support their calling (Amos 3:3). Pray today that your pastor and family take a vacation not related to work at least once a year (Mark 6:31). Ask the Lord how you might be a part of making a vacation happen.

Day 15

Pray that your pastor maintain a reasonable schedule, working hard for Christ and others (Proverbs 6:6). Pray that your pastor's work routine would honor God and be right for them and their ministry (Ecclesiastes 2:24). Pray that your pastor would be physically healthy, not mastered by food or drink (1 Timothy 4:8). Pray for your pastor's purity, that God help keep them from pornography and other sexual sin (Job 31:1; Philippians 4:8–9).

Day 16

Pray for the Lord to purify your pastor's will by clear and consistent application of the Word (Psalm 26:2). Pray that your pastor would begin each day connecting with God, strengthened by Scripture and prayer (5:3). Pray that your pastor would end each day connecting with God, repenting of sin and clinging to Jesus (3:5). Pray that your pastor would live each day connected to God in the joy of acceptance by our heavenly Father (Romans 5:1–2).

Day 17

Pray for your pastor's circle of friends, for close friends inside the church and outside (Proverbs 15:22). Pray that your pastor would join with a group of pastors in the community who pray for one another (Galatians 6:2). Pray for your pastor's professional growth, for the right gatherings for learning and fellowship (Proverbs 22:29). Pray for your pastor's sense of humor, for laughing easily at themselves and with others (Romans 12:3).

Day 18

Pray for your pastor's vision of ministry. Ask for focus on equipping others to serve (Ephesians 4:12). Pray for your pastor's goal of ministry, to make known the manifold wisdom of God (Ephesians 3:10). Pray that your pastor's vision and goals be prompted solely by the Holy Spirit and shape the mission and core values of the church (1 Corinthians 14).

Day 19

Pray that your pastor networks and gathers others to become partners in the ministry (1 Corinthians 12). Pray that your pastor values volunteers, that he equips and entrusts them with significant responsibilities (1 Corinthians 12:14; Ephesians 4:11). Pray that your pastor would cooperate appropriately with other churches and ministries (Mark 9:40). Pray that your pastor would rejoice when kingdom-minded churches and ministries do well (Romans 12:15).

Day 20

Pray for you pastor's preaching, that the Spirit use it to soften hearts and draw many to God (Hebrews 3:15). Pray for your pastor's preaching, that God use it to equip people for every good work (2 Timothy 3:17). Pray that as your pastor preaches, all who hear will be strengthened in their faith (Colossians 2:7).

Day 21

Pray that your pastor grows in faith and repentance as he prepares and preaches (Acts 20:20–21). Pray that your pastor's preaching would demolish arguments and capture thoughts for Christ (2 Corinthians 10:4–5). Pray that in your pastor's preaching, life and words match and that both set forth the truth (2 Corinthians 4:2).

Day 22

Pray for your pastor's leadership, that he would lead diligently and that others would recognize their calling, gifts, and skills (Romans 12:8). Pray that your pastor's leadership and life be exemplary, in speech, love, faith, and purity (1 Timothy 4:12). Pray that your pastor would be creative and innovative and be known as a problem solver (Proverbs 21:5), and that your pastor's leadership include wise and tempered counsel when considering change (19:2).

Day 23

Pray for your pastor's life management, for appropriate and godly responses to the unexpected (Proverbs 1:3), and for wisdom to prioritize and accomplish many tasks (Ephesians 5:16), and for physical, emotional, and spiritual health (1 Timothy 4:8). Pray that your pastor understands God's call to and from their church and for knowing their own seasons of life and ministry (Ecclesiastes 3:1).

Day 24

Pray for humility for your pastor, for a graceful approach in serving others (Proverbs 3:34). Pray for courage for your pastor, for a strong heart in the midst of conflict (Joshua 1:8–9). Pray for a teachable spirit for your pastor, for a deep desire to learn from God (Exodus 33:13). Pray for a servant's heart, for eagerness to care for the sheep (1 Peter 5:2). Pray for power for your pastor, that the Holy Spirit would enable him to be God's witness (Acts 1:8).

Day 25

Pray for purity for your pastor, for protection against virtual and physical sin (Matthew 5:28). Pray for rest for your pastor, for freedom from the bondage of overwork (Matthew 11:28–30). Pray for diligence for your pastor. Pray for a balance of grace and hard work (1 Corinthians 15:10). Pray for the authority of your pastor, for neither excess nor neglect, but joy (Hebrews 13:17).

Day 26

Pray for understanding for your pastor, for the correct words to make Christ known. Pray for boldness and clarity, that Jesus is the focus of every single sermon. Pray for your pastor's effectiveness and fruitfulness, that deep needs be met and lives be changed when they speak (Ephesians 6:19).

Day 27

Pray that your pastor be kept from unhealthy ambition, especially the numbers trap (John 12:43). Pray that your pastor be protected from both gossip and negative criticism (Proverbs 11:13). Ask that your pastor be kept from false expectations and undue burdens (Hebrews 13:17). Pray for freedom from strife, dissension, and weariness (Galatians 6:9).

Day 28

Pray for your pastor's time, for guarding against unnecessary conversations. Pray for your pastor's energy, for freedom from late meetings and too many commitments. Pray for your pastor's resolve, for guarding from stress, fatigue, and busyness (Ephesians 5:16). Pray for faithfulness for your pastor, for freedom from compulsions or addictions (1 Peter 5:8).

Day 29

Pray today for confidence for your pastor, for memory that security and hope are in Jesus alone (Romans 8:1). Pray for your pastor's mind, for guarding against futile thinking and vain ambition

(Ephesians 4:17). Pray also for your pastor's thinking, that every thought be captive to obey Christ (2 Corinthians 10:4–5).

Day 30

Pray for your pastor's health and well-being—for healing from grief caused by ministry. Pray for your pastor's joy, for a garment of praise instead of a spirit of despair (Isaiah 61:1–3). Pray for your pastor's rest and renewal, for rest of soul and joy of spirit in the yoke of Jesus (Matthew 11:29), and for pleasure in the grace that is new every morning (Lamentations 3:23).

Day 31

Pray for the scope of your pastor's work, in teaching and helping the weak and the poor, for no hesitation to teach anything that would be helpful, for service in public settings and from house to house. Pray for your pastor's clarity, that all must turn to God in repentance and faith in Jesus, and pray for your pastor's resolve, to finish the race and complete the task Jesus has given them (Acts 20:20–32).

Appendix C

Thirty-Five Practical Ways to Lovingly Support Your Pastor

It is our prayer that these thirty-five practical suggestions will help you and others in your congregation demonstrate love and support for your pastor and staff—and their families. The apostle Paul encourages us to help our leaders to be healthy:

> And now, friends, we ask you to honor those leaders who work so hard for you, who have been given the responsibility of urging and guiding you along in your obedience. Overwhelm them with appreciation and love! (1 Thessalonians 5:12–13 THE MESSAGE)

Support Your Church

- Take your place in the life of your church! Discover your spiritual gift and use it.
- Be a consistent Christian. Regularly attend and support the ministries of your church.
- Squelch gossip. If you hear a negative comment, respond with a positive one. If misinformation is

being spread, correct it with the accurate information. Or, if people are gossiping, just walk
away. Remember the Bible soundly condemns
gossip and careless speech.

- Continue to develop your own personal walk
  with the Lord—keep on growing.
- Make your own spouse and children your
  priority!
- Take an active part in at least one ministry of
  your church, giving help and/or leadership.
- Take the time to understand your pastor's personality, vision, and above all, their heart!
- Be teachable—be open to new thoughts and
  ideas.
- If you are not tithing, start working toward that
  goal, and then let your pastor know of your
  decision.
- Tell people about your church. Invite them to
  worship and introduce them to your pastor.
- Give new ideas a chance. "But we have always
  done it that way" are some of the most deflating
  words a creative pastor can hear.
- Remember—the amount of money you give does
  not buy you the right to be an antagonist in the
  church. Never presume that your faithful giving
  has purchased the pastor's ear.
- Share Christ in the marketplace, with neighbors
  and friends.

Care for Your Pastor

- Encourage your pastor in continuing education and spiritual enrichment, providing both time and finances.
- Make sure your pastor has a boss, trainer, coach, counselor, mentor, and friend (see *Survive or Thrive: Six Relationships Every Pastor Needs*, by Jimmy Dodd, David C Cook, 2015).
- Encourage your pastor to take risks. Give your pastor the freedom to launch a new program or implement a new idea that may appear outside the box.
- If possible, a membership to a health club is a wise investment for your pastor and staff.
- Never say negative things about your pastor or church in front of family or others. Talk directly to your pastor when you have concerns.
- A gift card to a restaurant or grocery store is deeply appreciated.
- A special gift (such as tickets to a sporting event or theater) can be a blessing. *Do not* give your pastor two tickets to the theater and then announce, "Actually I bought four tickets. My wife and I will be sitting next to you. Let's meet for dinner before the show. Our treat!" You have just turned a potential restful evening for a pastoral couple into a night of work.

- Help keep your pastor's technology relatively current and working well.

- Write a note telling your pastor something you learned from a recent sermon. A spoken compliment is always welcome, but a written one will be read over and over again for years. Additionally, write a letter to the church board sharing your appreciation for your pastor.

- Remember, pastors consider themselves to be caregivers. It may be hard for your pastor to receive care, so be relentless!

- Throw away the measuring stick. Don't expect that your pastor will do things the same way his predecessors did. Instead, focus on how your leader is being used by God to do effective ministry now.

- Purchase PastorCare+ for your pastor (www .pastorserve.net/pastorcareplus). This will provide a base level of coaching, care, and counseling for your pastor. The package also includes a three-night stay at a number of highly rated bed-and-breakfasts around the country.

- Purchase copies of *Pastors Are People Too* for friends who attend different churches. Challenge them to practically care for their pastor.

Care for Your Pastor's Family

- Protect the privacy of your pastor and family and their time together. Encourage your pastors to set boundaries to protect themselves, and then encourage others to honor those boundaries.
- Ministry is hard on marriages. Encourage your pastor and spouse to find and attend events that enrich marriage, then make finances available.
- Plan a surprise gift for your pastor and spouse— several days at a B&B will always be welcome!
- Encourage your pastor to take *all* of his or her vacation. Most pastors will not take all of their vacation because they lack the financial means to do so. If you have a vacation home, consider offering it to your pastor.
- Remember the birthdays and wedding anniversary of your pastor and family.
- Drop a note to your pastor's family to express appreciation and brighten their day.
- Remind yourself—and others in the church— the church is your pastor's secondary ministry. The pastor's family is your pastor's primary ministry.

Pray

- Pray daily for your pastor and family!
- Form a prayer group that prays regularly for your pastor and church.

*Adapted from *50 Ways to Love Your Pastor* by SonScape Retreats (available on www.sonscaperetreats.org).

Notes

Foreword

1. Thom S. Rainer, "Pastors and Mental Health," ThomRainer.com, February 26, 2014, http://thomrainer.com/2014/02/pastors-and-mental-health/; and Rainer, "How Many Hours Must a Pastor Work to Satisfy the Congregation," ThomRainer.com, July 24, 2013, http://thomrainer.com/2013/07/how-many -hours-must-a-pastor-work-to-satisfy-the-congregation/.

Introduction: Why the State of Pastors Should Matter to You

1. Peter Scazzero, *The Emotionally Healthy Church* (Grand Rapids, MI: Zondervan, 2003), 7.

2. These quotations are taken from the unpublished manuscript of *A Reason to Hope* by Jerry and Nancy Walsh. Used by permission of the authors.

Chapter 2: Twenty-Four-Hour Pastor

1. Jim Anderson, "Tale of Two Oswalds," writing some years ago in a newsletter for the Evangelical Free Church of America North Central District. The details of the newsletter have been lost to time, but the author (Larry Magnuson) corresponded with him regarding quoting this material.

2. J. Oswald Sanders, "Lessons I Have Learned," *Discipleship Journal* 3 (1983): 14, emphasis mine.

Chapter 3: Pastor Superman

1. "Unreasonable," Dictionary.com, dictionary.reference.com/browse/unreasonable?s=t (accessed September 2, 2015).

Chapter 4: Capacity

1.   Gloria Mark, *Gallup Business Journal*, June 8, 2006.

2.   C. S. Lewis, *They Stand Together: The Letters of C. S. Lewis to Arthur Greeves* (1914–1963), ed. Walter Hooper (New York: MacMillan, 1979), 499.

3.   Madeleine L'Engle, *Walking on Water: Reflections on Faith and Art* (Colorado Springs: WaterBrook, 2001), 109.

Chapter 8: The Pastor's Family

1.   "Discerning Positive Character Qualities through Negative Behavior Traits," KathieNelson.com, www.kathienelson.com/wp-content/uploads/Discerning-Positive-Qualities-v5.pdf (accessed September 7, 2015).

PastorServe Book Series

The PastorServe Book Series is dedicated to grace-centered, timeless books for pastors, ministry leaders, and church leadership ministering in a variety of settings in locations around the world. These books expose and address critical issues in pastoral ministry with an emphasis on the relentless love of Jesus. The series focuses on both the front stage and the back stage of pastoral ministry in order to help the reader bring their entire life into alignment with the gospel of Jesus Christ. PastorServe was started by Jimmy and Sally Dodd in 1999 in order that no pastor would walk alone.

Survive or Thrive: Six Relationships
Every Pastor Needs

Pastors Are People Too: What They Won't
Tell You but You Need to Know

Watch for more PastorServe titles coming soon!

About the Authors

Larry Magnuson is president of SonScape Retreats. A graduate of Bethel University (BA) and North Park Seminary (MDiv), he is the founding pastor of Maple Grove Covenant Church in Minneapolis, Minnesota. Over the last fifteen years Larry and his wife, Barbara, have led two hundred weeklong retreats for pastors and their spouses, as well as working with Christian leaders on five different continents. They are blessed with four children, two sons-in-law, a daughter-in-law, and five grandchildren. Living high in the mountains of Colorado in a one-hundred-year-old log cabin, Larry enjoys hiking, fishing, Jeep riding, and sitting quietly with Barbara looking off into the mountains with a cup of coffee in hand.

Jimmy Dodd is founder and president of PastorServe. A graduate of Wheaton College (BA) and Gordon-Conwell Theological Seminary (MDiv), he pastored in Chicago, Boston, Greenville (South Carolina), Kansas City, and Colorado Springs, where he served for ten years on the teaching team of Woodmen Valley Chapel. Jimmy is the author of *Survive or Thrive: Six Relationships Every Pastor Needs*. A well-known speaker, Jimmy has had the privilege of making more than 125 trips to train leaders in third-world countries. In 2000, he helped launch Cross International, a ministry devoted to serving the poorest of the poor. Jimmy and his wife, Sally, have five children, one daughter-in-law, and one granddaughter. Two of their daughters were adopted from China. In his spare time, Jimmy can be found with his family, walking his dog, Murphy, or at Allen Fieldhouse in Lawrence, Kansas, cheering on his beloved Jayhawks.

SonScape Retreats Summary

For over thirty years, SonScape Retreats has been used by God to transform the lives, marriages, and ministries of pastors and Christian leaders. The weeklong, small-group, safe, and confidential retreats are uniquely designed to address the personal issues of each couple or single, as well as providing the tools for ongoing health in life and ministry. Amazing retreat settings in Colorado, Tennessee, and upstate New York set the stage for God to bring healing, rest, renewal, and life change to the men and women called to lead His church. For more information on SonScape Retreats or to register your pastor for a retreat, visit our website at www.sonscape.org.

PastorServe Summary

PastorServe's vision is that every pastor would have a pastor. The organization exists so that no pastor would walk alone. In an effort to help the church reach its full redemptive potential, PastorServe works across denominational lines to support, encourage, train, equip, coach, and consult with pastors across the country. Founded in 1999, PastorServe has been recognized as one of the leading organizations today that helps pastors and churches navigate the challenges they face—both during the seasons of crisis and noncrisis. Believing that every pastor needs a pastor, PastorServe would be honored to journey with you in safe and confidential ways.

You can learn more about PastorServe by visiting their website at www.pastorserve.org.

PastorServe ... *Because Every Pastor Needs a Pastor*